ROUTLEDGE LIBRA
EDUCATION AN

Volume 14

LEARNING LIBERATION

LEARNING LIBERATION
Women's Response to Men's Education

JANE L. THOMPSON

Routledge
Taylor & Francis Group

LONDON AND NEW YORK

First published in 1983 by Croom Helm

This edition first published in 2017
by Routledge
2 Park Square, Milton Park, Abingdon, Oxon OX14 4RN

and by Routledge
711 Third Avenue, New York, NY 10017

Routledge is an imprint of the Taylor & Francis Group, an informa business

British Library Cataloguing in Publication Data
A catalogue record for this book is available from the British Library

ISBN: 978-1-138-73736-5 (Set)
ISBN: 978-1-315-18103-5 (Set) (ebk)
ISBN: 978-1-138-04034-2 (Volume 14) (hbk)
ISBN: 978-1-138-04038-0 (Volume 14) (pbk)
ISBN: 978-1-315-17516-4 (Volume 14) (ebk)

Publisher's Note
The publisher has gone to great lengths to ensure the quality of this reprint but
points out that some imperfections in the original copies may be apparent.

Disclaimer
The publisher has made every effort to trace copyright holders and would welcome
correspondence from those they have been unable to trace.

Learning Liberation

WOMEN'S RESPONSE TO MEN'S EDUCATION

Jane L. Thompson

CROOM HELM
London & Canberra

© 1983 Jane L. Thompson
Croom Helm Ltd, Provident House, Burrell Row,
Beckenham, Kent BR3 1AT

British Library Cataloguing in Publication Data

Thompson, Jane
  Learning liberation.—(Radical Forum of adult
  education)
  1. Women's studies
  I. Title   II. Series
  305.4   HQ1180
ISBN 0-7099-2414-3
ISBN 0-7099-2439-9 Pbk

Filmset in Great Britain by
Patrick and Anne Murphy Typesetters
Highcliffe-on-Sea, Dorset

Printed and bound in Great Britain by
Biddles Ltd, Guildford and King's Lynn

CONTENTS

FOR STRONG WOMEN
and for
THOSE OF US WHO ARE
BECOMING STRONGER

The purpose of this series is to provide a forum of discussion for the whole field of adult and continuing education. With increasing pressure on traditional areas of secondary and higher education and changing employment patterns, there is a growing awareness that the continuing education of adults has a vital role to play in our society. All the books in the series are about radical thinking and practice in education in Britain and abroad. The authors are concerned with education in its widest sense and, by implication, with the inadequacy of traditional views of education as a process which concerns only the young and which takes place only in the formal sectors.

A major focus of the series is on the consequences of social change and the need to formulate an educational response to new technologies and new economic, social and political conditions as they affect *all* members of our society. The growth and distribution of knowledge is rapidly making traditional models of education obsolete, and new learning technologies are being developed which give a greater potential than ever before to the possibilities of education as an instrument of social change, but only if we change radically our conceptions of education itself, and adopt a critical view of the uses to which it could be put.

At the same time that educational ideals become more attainable through the growth of knowledge and learning technologies, economic, social, political, sexual and racial conflicts remain undiminished, and often find expression in educational inequalities and injustices. The series aims to explore this paradox, to identify obstacles in the way of realising the full potential of education for all, and to describe some of the initiatives being taken in the United Kingdom and abroad to try to overcome them.

Jane Thompson has written a brave and radical book which not only dissects the intrinsic and oppressive sexism of conventional adult and continuing education, but which argues the case for women-centred education with a powerful and compelling logic. It is a rare book within the literature of adult education, mixing provocative theories with details of practice in a wide-ranging and readable debate. It will speak naturally to all concerned, either as

1

teachers or students, with the process through which women's rights to educational equality can be guaranteed. It is an outspoken book, challenging and controversial to those who usually monopolise ideas in adult and continuing education, but which speaks with honesty and conviction and a serious commitment to transforming the relationships which presently dehumanise both women and men. It makes me, as one who has been involved in the education of women for almost a decade, ashamed of my compromises; but I am proud to have commissioned and to be associated with this book.

Jo Campling
(Jo Campling is Lecturer in Social Policy, Hillcroft College)

PREFACE

The question facing Women's Studies today is the extent to which she has, in the last decade, matured into the dutiful daughter of the white patriarchal university — a daughter who threw tantrums and played the tomboy when she was younger, but who has now learned to wear a dress and speak and act almost as nicely as Daddy wants her to. And the extent to which Women's Studies can remember that her mother was not Athena, but the Women's Liberation Movement, a grass roots political movement with roots in the Civil Rights movement of the 1960s; a movement blazing with lesbian energy whose earliest journals had names like *It Ain't Me Babe, No More Fun and Games, Off Our Backs, Up From Under* and *The Furies*. In other words, how disobedient will Women's Studies be in the 1980s? And how will she address the racism, misogyny, homophobia of the university and of the corporate society in which it is embedded? And how will feminist scholars and teachers choose to practise their disobedience to white patriarchy?[1]

A book which is about the meaning and significance of women's education cannot fail to respond to Adrienne Rich's questions, for they are central to the issues which confront feminist teachers and scholars. They also demand a response which is offered primarily to women, for it is women's education and women's control of it that I am concerned about. If men wish to understand, or care to be persuaded, the arguments are here for their consideration, but a book which merely succeeds in impressing or pleasing men, and which says nothing relevant to women searching for authentic knowledge and a women-centred education committed to and controlled by women, is a book for others to write.

It is usual within the male academic tradition to objectify the subject matter of research and publication;[2] and whilst it is important to take from the masculine intellectual tradition those ingredients which will enable us, as women, to equip ourselves with the knowledge, skills and perspectives we need to define ourselves wisely, we certainly have no wish to become the objects of our own subjectivity.

3

The style most frequently chosen to discuss adult and continuing education initiatives relies heavily on quantitative data gathered, with an illusion of objectivity, *about* human beings rather than *for* them. Institutional practices are described, curriculum options itemised, policy recommendations explored and teaching methods evaluated. Any glimmer of insight gets drowned in jargon, charts and footnotes — strangled by professional defensiveness. There is rarely if ever the sense of learning happening, of the passions which motivate the learners or the crystallisation of ideas and feelings which can challenge and empower both students and teachers alike. The essence of education is not a neutral, narrowly instrumental, separate from life activity — though some would persuade us that it should be — but a powerful political weapon which serves either to reinforce and bolster the logic of the present system or helps us to engage in the pursuit of freedom.

Any discussion about education which ignores questions of political purpose and control is hardly worth having, particularly for feminists. For we women the key issues in education are not about academic excellence or in denying our access to institutions created and controlled by men, but about securing our position in an education system which takes our concerns, our questions, our needs and our strengths as women completely seriously. And this will mean, as we shall see, a very different kind of system.

It will also mean a different kind of discussion from the usual analysis of adult and continuing education. For the intention here is not to describe women's education as an object of interest, but to illuminate the process through which women, against considerable odds, are learning liberation. In this respect what we women know of education from our own experience as students and teachers is central to the discussion — allegations of emotional and unrigorous scholarship notwithstanding. Subjective experience is the starting point for any validation of theory. Theory which can inform and enhance practice will be useful only if it grows out of practice and makes sense to the lived experience of the practitioners. Its purpose is to clarify and strengthen our process of becoming, not to freeze our possibilities at the moment of definition. And its responsibility is to be true to the realities of those who make it — which might be quite contrary to the realities of those who would like us to see things differently.

Notes

1. Adrienne Rich, address to the National Women's Studies of America Annual Conference, June 1981.
2. Helen Roberts (ed.), *Doing Feminist Research*, RKP, 1981.

ACKNOWLEDGEMENTS

My thanks to Brynderwen for giving me the space to write; to the many women whose words are included here among my own; to Helen and my friends, especially Judith and Sheila, for their love and support.

FOR STRONG WOMEN

A strong woman is a woman who is straining
A strong woman is a woman standing
on tiptoe and lifting a barbell
while trying to sing Boris Godunov.
A strong woman is a woman at work
cleaning out the cesspool of the ages
and while she shovels, she talks about
how she doesn't mind crying, it opens
the ducts of the eyes, and throwing up
develops the stomach muscles, and
she goes on shovelling with tears in her nose.

A strong woman is a woman in whose head
a voice is repeating, I told you so,
ugly, bad girl, bitch, nag, shrill, witch,
ballbuster, nobody will ever love you back,
why aren't you feminine, why aren't you
soft, why aren't you quiet, why aren't you dead?

A strong woman is a woman determined
to do something others are determined
not to be done. She is pushing up on the bottom
of a lead coffin lid. She is trying to raise a
manhole cover with her head, she is trying
to butt her way through a steel wall.
Her head hurts. People waiting for the hole
to be made say, hurry, you're so strong.

A strong woman is a woman bleeding
inside. A strong woman is a woman making
herself strong every morning while her teeth
loosen and her back throbs. Every baby,
a tooth, midwives used to say, and now
every battle a scar. A strong woman
is a mass of scar tissue that aches
when it rains and wounds that bleed
when you bump them and memories that get up
in the night and pace in boots to and fro.

A strong woman is a woman who craves love
like oxygen or she turns blue choking.
A strong woman is a woman who loves
strongly and weeps strongly and is strongly
terrified and has strong needs. A strong woman
is strong in words, in action, in connection, in feeling;
she is not strong as a stone but as a wolf suckling
her young. Strength is not in her, but she
enacts it as the wind fills a sail.

What comforts her is others loving
her equally for the strength and for the weakness
from which it issues, lightning from a cloud.
Lightning stuns. In rain, the clouds disperse.
Only water of connection remains, flowing through us.
Strong is what we make each other. Until we are all
strong together, a strong woman is a woman strongly afraid.

Marge Piercy

1 THE RE-EMERGENCE OF FEMINISM

When Betty Friedan wrote *The Feminine Mystique* in 1963 she talked of 'the problem with no name':

> The problem lay buried, unspoken, for many years in the minds of American women. It was a strange stirring, a sense of dissatisfaction, a yearning that women suffered in the middle of the twentieth century United States. Each suburban wife struggled with it alone. As she made the beds, shopped for groceries, matched slipover material, ate peanut butter sandwiches with her children, chauffered Cub Scouts and Brownies, lay beside her husband at night — she was afraid to ask even the silent question — 'Is this all?'

Twenty years later we have come a long way. The problem has been named, and we have a movement and the makings of a theory. The problem is male supremacy, described by Ann Popkin as:

> The institutional, all-encompassing power that men have as a group over women, the systematic exclusion of women from power in the society, and the systematic devaluation of all roles and traits which society has assigned to women.[1]

The solution to our problem is not, of course, to become more confident, less apologetic, more 'uppity', less passive, more self-reliant, less guilt-ridden — although we need to be all of these as well — but to challenge and confront the male supremacy which has institutionalised our inequality,

Fresh from the Civil Right Movement, student politics and the New Left as we were, inspiration for the theoretical work we had to do seemed to be in Marxist and socialist explanations of class oppression; for here were definitions of the world which very convincingly described the origins and ramifications of exploitation.

But the conventional wisdom of the New Left brought little comfort. So long as the relationships of production and class oppression were the focus of attention, the relationships of

9

reproduction and oppression based on gender were discounted variously as bourgeois, divisive, irrelevant and atheoretical. Come the revolution and all would be well. Get rid of capitalist relations of production, liberate the working class, and women, like their brothers, would inherit an altogether better world. This is probably true, but would it be a more equal world? Stokely Carmichael's advice to black women is apocryphal — their position in the revolution was 'prone', and innumerable speeches beginning with 'The Black Man . . .' make it quite clear for whom liberation was intended. For the women who made the tea whilst the men of Black Power and the New Left planned their revolution, there seemed not very much to build upon in terms of sexual equality for the brave new world to come. Women working in the socialist and grass-roots political movements of the left were faced more and more with two main problems. Lydia Sargent[2] identifies them as:

(1) The problem of day-to-day work (who cleans the office/ who messes it up, who writes the leaflets/who types them, who talks in meetings/who takes notes, who gains status through sexual relations/who gives status through sexual relations;
(2) The problem of theory (who leads the revolution, who makes it, who is liberated by it, and who keeps the home fires burning during it).

It didn't take long for women to discover the answers to the problems of theory and day-to-day work.

White Marxism defined the answer to the first question, sexist males the answer to the second. That is workers at the point of production (read white, working-class males) will make the revolution led by a revolutionary cadre of politicos (read middle-class, white males steeped in economic theory). Women (mostly white) would keep the home fires burning during it, functioning as revolutionary nurturers/secretaries; typing, filing, phoning, feeding, healing, supporting, loving and occasionally even participating on the front lines as quasi-revolutionary cheer leaders. At the same time that suburban women read and identified with Friedan's 'problem with no name', women in the New Left were busy cleaning and decorating movement offices, cooking movement dinners, handling day care, chauffering activists to demonstrations, typing letters and leaflets, answering phones, and lying beside their movements' lovers and husbands at night, also afraid to ask the silent question; 'Is this all?'

It became crucial, Sargent continues, given this nightmare vision, for women to work in a different way if they were to become more than 'the sex objects for their revolutionary "brothers".'

A new term named the problem and helped to encapsulate the ubiquity of male power over women historically, economically, psychologically, ideologically and physically. Patriarchy — literally defined as 'the power of the father' — was used increasingly to describe the explicit and implicit subordination of women by the rule of men. Just as capital exploited and appropriated the labour power of waged workers at the point of production, it was argued, so did patriarchy exploit and appropriate the gratuitous labour of women in the home and in the relationships of reproduction. Marion Scott[3] puts its focus in a nutshell: 'Within the family labour is replenished, sexuality is controlled and sex roles are acquired. It is a powerful institution and the site of women's subordination'.

All men, whatever their social position, both before capitalism and despite its modification in state socialist societies, exercise this oppression and share a very real interest in ensuring its preservation. For emerging theorists of the women's movement, like Christine Delphy in France, patriarchy was named as the main enemy[4] which did not confine its oppression to the home front. From the relationships of reproduction and the sexual division of labour in the home develops a whole series of related repressions in which men have colluded historically to deny women public office, legal rights, equal consideration as productive workers, control over their own health and welfare, and the right to define their own sexuality. Gradually, theories emerged about the material basis of women's oppression, the relevance of class in the oppression of women, the links between the oppression of women and other oppressed groups. But although there is a good deal of agreement among feminists about the problem of patriarchy, there are a number of theoretical responses depending on whether feminists are also Marxists, socialists or radicals.

Radical feminists believe the main problem is gender — that oppression based on the sexual division of labour predates and even predetermines the division of labour by class and race. Marxist feminists emphasise that 'women' are more significantly 'workers' and have borrowed the language and analyses of conventional

Marxism to make connections with domestic labour. Socialist feminists, like Marxists, recognise that class oppression structures the exploitation of all workers, but that patriarchy acts as a parallel system of oppression controlling women. Both forms of oppression come together in the operation of the state, so that the state is both a class state and a patriarchal state.

The different emphases lead to theoretical and strategic wrangles. Marxists accuse radicals and socialists of being insufficiently materialist and not sufficiently aware of class discrepancies in the position of women. Radicals criticise Marxists and socialists for their naïvety about patriarchy and its apparent need psychologically and even physically, to coerce women whatever the economic conditions might be. Socialists accuse Marxists of being too economistic, and radicals for being too subjective. Black feminists accuse all three of being racist; and lesbian feminists point out to women who are not lesbians the oppressive nature of compulsive heterosexuality.

When it comes to taking action, Marxists and socialists emphasise the need to make strategic allegiances with the male left, whilst also organising separately around specific campaigns. Radicals are more likely to advocate autonomous action and political separatism from association with male oppressors.

Michèle Barratt and Mary McIntosh[5] complain that 'in Britain there has been a curious reluctance to take up these issues in an explicit and theoretical way'; and Kuhn and Wolpe[6] agree that our theoretical delineation of questions about the nature of women's oppression is as yet at a very preliminary stage.

But at the same time as academic feminists have been struggling theoretically with explanations of our oppression and discussing strategic possibilities, others have been making the connections in our daily lives about how we experience and can resist patriarchy. The women's movement is essentially a grass-roots movement, with no official leaders, headquarters, membership scheme or bureaucracy. Its members are all those women who recognise the oppressive consequences of male supremacy and who, in a variety of settings, and within a number of different but related campaigns, are organising our resistance.

Women fighting for equal rights at work and within trade unions, for freedom from male violence, for changes in the law, for control over their own fertility and sexuality, for better child-care provision, and better education, are all, in different ways, engaged in the same process of liberation — a process which actually and potentially involves the consciousness and energy of millions of women in every country of the world. And it is this movement — international, independent and important — which, when we talk about women's adult and continuing education, has to be taken considerably more seriously than is presently appreciated by the policy-makers and opinion leaders who currently prepare programmes and provide classes.

Notes

1. Ann Popkin, 'The Personal is Political: The Women's Liberation Movement', in Dick Cluster (ed.) *They Should Have Served That Cup of Coffee*, Southend Press, 1979.

2. Lydia Sargent, 'New Left Women and Men: The Honeymoon is Over', in Lydia Sargent (ed.) *Women and Revolution: The Unhappy Marriage of Marxism and Feminism*, Pluto Press, 1981.

3. Marion Scott, 'Teach Her a Lesson: Sexist Curriculum in Patriarchal Education', in Dale Spender and Elizabeth Sarah (eds) *Learning to Lose*, The Women's Press, 1980.

4. Christine Delphy, 'The Main Enemy: A Materialist Analysis of Women's Oppression', WRRC publication: *Explanations in Feminism*, no. 3, 1977.

5. Michèle Barratt and Mary McIntosh, 'Christine Delphy: Towards a Materialist Feminism', *Feminist Review* 1, 1979.

6. Annette Kuhn and Annmarie Wolpe (eds) *Feminism and Materialism: Women and Modes of Production*, RKP, 1978.

2 THE POLITICS OF WOMEN'S OPPRESSION

I've had enough
I'm sick of seeing and touching
Both sides of things
Sick of being the damn bridge for everybody

Nobody
Can talk to anybody
Without me
Right?

I explain my mother to my father and my father to my
little sister
My little sister to my brother my brother to the white feminists
The white feminists to the black church folks the black church
  folks
To the ex-hippies the ex-hippies to the black separatists the
Black separatists to the artists the artists to my friends parents
  . . .

Then
I've got to explain myself
To everybody

I do more translating
Than the Gawdamn U.N.

Forget it
I'm sick of it

I'm sick of filling in your gaps

Sick of being your insurance against
The isolation of your self imposed limitations
Sick of being the crazy at your holiday dinners
Sick of being the odd one at your Sunday brunches
Sick of being the sole Black friend to 34 individual white
  people

Find another connection to the rest of the world
Find something else to make you legitimate
Find some other way to be political and hip

I will not be the bridge to your womanhood
Your manhood
Your human-ness

I'm sick of reminding you not to
Close off too tight for too long

I'm sick of mediating with your worst self
On behalf of your better selves

I am sick
Of having to remind you
To breathe
Before you suffocate
Your own fool self

Forget it
Stretch or drown
Evolve or die

The bridge I must be
Is the bridge to my own power
I must translate
My own fears
Mediate
My own weaknesses

I must be the bridge to nowhere
But my true self
And then
I will be useful

Donna Kate Rushin[1]

Caught between conflicting claims and other people's expectations, walked over like a bridge between competing interests, the fight for this black woman to be true to herself before she can be properly useful to others, echoes the struggle of all women for integrity, autonomy and wholeness. Within each woman there is knowledge: energy and power which exists but which, because of the rule of men, has frequently been displaced, buried and confused. Patriarchy has kept us like a handmaiden to its interests, totally preoccupied with the servicing of its concerns, bereft of our own identity as we become incorporated within its peculiar logic. Patriarchy has rewarded us for our complicity and docility, kept us isolated and separate from each other, and has prevented us from making the bridges between our emotional experiences and social conditions which once connected contain the seeds of revolutionary change.

The struggle 'to be whole' and the concern 'to make authentic bridges' are both simple and profound comments on what should be the major preoccupation of women learning liberation. In a world in which women own only one-hundredth of the wealth and do two-thirds of the work for one-tenth of the wages; in which men monopolise public power in government, law, industry, commerce, science, culture, education and religion; and in which discrimination on the basis of gender is arguably the most socially acceptable form of oppression, a casual observer may be forgiven for attributing some kind of genetic defect which has prevented half of the population of the world from achieving at least parity of esteem with the other half. But women's oppression is not a problem of biology, it is a problem of history — of the interplay between materialism and patriarchy.

And the task of the women's movement now, as perhaps it always has been, is to understand and explain the circumstances in which women have been systematically subjected to male authority, to check with each other about the experiences and conditions of this subjection; and to generate the knowledge, the creative anger, and the energy which can transform our relationships with one another and with men, which can resist patriarchal power and which can bring about change.

The women's movement has always had a strong educational component, in the sense that liberation has to be learned as well as created; but it has never been a merely intellectual affair. The awakening of ideas, the encoding of experience, and the generation of energy has always been linked to forms of personal action and public campaigns. The intention has always been to take increasing control over our own lives as women and to bring about the destruction of patriarchal power bases in the wider society. An important and unique principle has been the link between the personal and the political.

In this respect, as Donna Kate Rushin's poem makes clear, we have to make bridges to our own power, to find ways of 'defining our own identity'. Some indication of the enormity of being free to conceive of ourselves separate from the impositions of vested male interests, without the legacy of years of patriarchal conditioning, and uncontrolled by the kinds of social imperatives based on prejudice which effectively keep us in our place, became clear to me when a woman I know asked 'If I discover my own identity, when will I know that I've found it?' So much did she feel herself to be the creation of other people that she doubted she could ever recognise an alternative. So long as men control the knowledge we have about ourselves, mediate the information they want us to take seriously, retain economic control over us and monitor our progress and performance according to their tastes and inclinations — we have little space to discover our own true selves. But once this is appreciated, when 'the penny drops', so to speak, and the ubiquity of the ploys used to delude and distract us from the discovery of ourselves are revealed, it becomes significantly easier to recognise and act upon the priority of recreating ourselves and each other in an altogether different way.

If an important part of wholeness is the fight for an identity which emotionally, intellectually and politically learns not to be fragmented by patriarchal assaults on our integrity, and from which all dishonest allegiances and false dependances born of guilt, fear and lies[2] are exorcised; then another part is the search for cultural wholeness — the recognition that as women we have a past and a heritage worth reclaiming.

Men have a continuity of culture and recorded wisdom which enables them to speak with their ancestors, and to learn from their mistakes and advances in a way which shapes and informs their present deliberations. Women lack this continuity, and each new generation has to confront afresh the same hard lessons learned by our foremothers.

The elimination of women's culture, particularly black women's culture, from the records does not mean that it does not exist — merely that men have made it disappear.[3]

The struggles women experience today may take different forms, but they are, of course, not new. Women have been subordinate to men and oppressed by them in many different sorts of societies. Neither is the oppression of women a temporary phenomenon. The rule of men certainly existed long before capitalism developed, and has shown little evidence of withering away with the introduction of communism and socialism. But for as long as women have been subjected to the rule of men there have been those who have resisted its authority. To find evidence of women's protests at the omnipotence of male power we could return to Mary Wollstonecraft (1759–97), who in 1792 published *A Vindication of the Rights of Women*; or to Aphra Benn (1640–89) who had seventeen plays published in 17 years, who wrote thirteen novels 30 years before the male literary tradition 'invented' novels,[4] and who faced continual carping from male critics because she spoke neither Latin nor Greek. We could return to Harriet Martineau (1802–76), who was well aware of the 'evils and disadvantages of the imperfect institution of marriage' in which women continued to be 'ill-educated, passive and subserviant', and who declared in her auto-biography (1877) 'I am in truth very thankful for not having married at all'.

We could look to those women in America and Britain who argued for equality and the vote. Angelina Grimké (1805–79) writing to Catherine Beecher in 1836 argued passionately for equal rights as a prerequisite to human rights,

> Our fathers waged a bloody conflict with England because they were taxed without being represented. They were not willing to be governed by laws they had no voice in making; but this is the way women are governed in this republic.

Elizabeth Cady Stanton (1815–1902) knew women 'had souls large enough to feel the wrongs of others' and in pressing the struggle for the vote declared that by

> standing alone we learned our power; we repudiated man's counsels for evermore; and solemnly vowed that there should never be another season of silence until we had the same rights everywhere on this green earth, as man.

When Sojourner Truth spoke on the issue of suffrage in 1867 she knew that black women face both racism and sexism:

I feel that if I had to answer for the deeds done in my body just as much as a man, I have a right to have just as much as a man. There is a great stir about the colored men getting their rights, but not a word about the colored women; and if colored men get their rights, and not colored women theirs, you see the colored men will be masters over the women, and it will be just as bad as it was before. So I am for keeping the thing going while things are stirring, because if we wait 'til it is still it will take a great long while to get it going again.

In Britain Emily Pankhurst declared 'I am what you call a hooligan'. Seeing that men cared far more for property than for human life and nothing for legalistic arguments about women's suffrage, she claimed no moral commitment to the laws they introduced to prevent suffragette agitation and civil disobedience. She encouraged her sisters to be bold.

You have to make more noise than anybody else, you have to make yourself more obtrusive than anybody else, you have to fill all the papers more than anybody else, in fact you have to be there all the time and see that they do not snow you under, if you are really going to get your reform realised.

We could look to Hubertine Auclert (1848–1914) in France, or Ch'iu Chin (1874–1907) in China or Aleksandra Kollantai (1872–1952) in Russia for the same energy and conviction.

In the late seventeenth and eighteenth centuries the rights of women to education, and opposition to marriage as an arrangement of property and ownership were frequently discussed in pamphlets and journalistic literature. In 1697 Mary Astell, author of *A Serious Proposal to the Ladies*, advocated separate education for women in which they could become learned, free from the interference of men.[5] In 1790 Catherine Macaulay wrote a book on women's education which

assumed that sex differences could be accounted for in terms of socialisation (particularly education) and that the 'natural' superiority of men was not natural at all but a product of their own control and 'engineering'.[6]

And all this at a time when in the seventeenth century thousands of women in Britain and Europe were persecuted and killed as witches — mainly for being old and poor or acting as midwives and wisewomen; and when in the nineteenth century women were still being drawn to market by their husbands, with halters round their necks, to be auctioned like cattle to the highest bidder.

These are just some of the women we know who shared our struggle and who shared our anger. There are other countless thousands whose names and individual battles are lost to us. Elizabeth Janeway has commented[7] 'American women are not the only people in the world who manage to lose track of themselves, but we seem to mislay the past in a singularly absentminded fashion'. Part of the explanation lies in the fact that 'like their personal lives, women's history is fragmented, interrupted: a shadow history of human beings whose existence has been shaped by the efforts and the demands of others'. But more significant, perhaps, is the recognition that 'We have been stating our case for centuries, without continuity . . . while generation after generation of women have protested often vehemently and to a wide audience — these words have "disappeared" '.[8]

The reason according to Dorothy Smith[9] is straightforward. Men have paid attention only to the concerns of other men.

> The circle of men whose writing and talk was significant to each other extends backwards in time as far as our records reach. What men were doing was relevant to men, was written about men, by men, for men. Men listened and listen to what one another said.

So long as men have written the history books and controlled 'the general currency of thought' the philosophy and agitation, the poetry and literature, the art and the politics of women have been obliterated from the records.

The delight with which each new generation of feminists uncovers the bravery and wisdom of our foremothers, and discovers in their journals and letters and books and pamphlets totally relevant commentary about the position of women today written a hundred, 200, 300 years ago is important; it is a bridge to the past, a heritage and a culture from which we can grow and learn and struggle to become whole. But the discovery is tempered by the clear recognition that this is a heritage which we have had to search out and reclaim and rescue from virtual extinction. It has been subject to a process of deletion which continues to persist so long as men control the selection, confirmation and distribution of that which counts as worthwhile knowledge. All the more reason then why we women must learn to validate and generate our own knowledge, much as men have done — albeit in a different way and for a different purpose — so that lessons of the past can inform the experience of the present, in the expectation that we shall inherit a world which is more of our own making than the one we shall acquire from men.

More than the suppression of women's culture in the past and the ignorance with which we as women begin to anticipate our future, is the problem of making authentic bridges between the diverse conditions of our present lived experiences. An important concern of the women's movement is its intention to take seriously the feelings of all women and to accommodate the similarity, variety, diversity and contradictions of our different experiences of the world. And yet as women we have very real problems in doing this without repeating the same oppressive behaviour of those who have subordinated us. This is especially true in relation to race, sexuality and class. For the women writing in *This Bridge Called My Back*,[10] the lived experience of racism is more important than the experience of sexism. Black activist women in Britain also define their primary oppression as racism rather than gender. Black women face a double oppression — that of race *and* sex. Lorraine Bethel[11] puts it like this:

> The codification of Blackness by whites and males is seen in the terms 'Thinking like a woman' and 'acting like a nigger' which are based on the premises that there are typically black and female ways of thinking and acting. Therefore the most pejorative concept in the white/male world view would be that of thinking and acting like a 'nigger woman'.

But whilst black males may be allies in the struggle against racism, their reaction to feminism is notoriously hostile and their view of women essentially sexist. This is how a black nationalist pamphlet of the 1970s defines male and female roles.

We understand that it is and has been traditional that the man is the head of the house. He is the leader of the house/nation because his knowledge of the world is broader, his awareness is greater, his understanding is fuller and his application of this information is wiser . . . after all, it is only reasonable that the man be the head of the house because he is able to defend and protect the development of his home . . . women cannot do the same things as men — they are made by nature to function differently. Equality of men and women is something which cannot happen even in the abstract world. Men are not equal to other men, i.e. ability, experience or even understanding. The value of men and women can be seen as in the value of gold and silver — they are not equal but both have great value. We must realise that men and women are a complement to each other because there is no house/family without a man and his wife. Both are essential to the development of any life.[12]

For women of all races and different classes patriarchy acts as 'the enemy within', but for black women it would be wrong to ignore the implications of discrimination *within* discrimination. Women as blacks and as black women are at 'the bottom' so far as white capitalist patriarchy is concerned — as such the specific struggle of black women is revolutionary in implication.

If Black women were free, it would mean that everyone else would have to be free since [their] freedom would necessitate the destruction of all the systems of oppression.[13]

Sadly the women's movement, white and middle class in origin, has repeatedly failed to appreciate this or to acknowledge its own racism. For those of us who emerged from the radical politics of the sixties and the New Left, and regrouped around the concerns of sexual politics, our understanding of Afro—American, Puerto Rican, Asian or West Indian women's lives is infinitesimal. At best our liberal humanism can idealise a future in which skin colour will not matter. But this is of little consolation, I suspect, or indeed much relevance, to those who live each day with racism.

Judit Moshkovich[14] makes clear that 'When Anglo-American women speak of developing a new feminist or women's culture, they are still working or thinking within an Anglo-American cultural framework'. Anglo-American women are totally saturated in western white culture, with little knowledge or respect for the cultures of Third World people. Also a lot of Third World women are ignorant about each other. We need as women to confront our own ignorance and racism rather than be distracted by the ascribed pathology of cultures we do not understand.

Since the re-emergence of the women's movement, particularly in Europe and North America, we have educated ourselves considerably, but we have done little to learn about our differences, white and black.

Audre Lorde[15] is clear that,

In a world of possibility for us all, our personal visions help lay the groundwork for political action. The failure of (white) feminists to recognise difference as a crucial strength is a failure to reach beyond the first patriarchal lesson. Divide and conquer, in our world, must become define and empower . . . *For the masters tools will never dismantle the masters house.* They allow us temporarily to beat him at his own game, but they will never allow us to bring about genuine change. (Lorde's italics)

For a woman to be a lesbian in a male-dominated, capitalist, heterosexist, misogynist, homophobic, racist and imperialist society like Britain or North America is, as Cheryl Clarke[16] points out, an act of supreme resistance.

No matter how a woman lives out her lesbianism — in the closet, in the state legislature, in the bedroom — she has rebelled against becoming a male-defined female and this rebellion is dangerous business in patriarchy.

As Adrienne Rich[17] makes clear, lesbianism pre-dates feminism.

Before any kind of feminist movement existed, or could exist, lesbianism existed: women who loved women, who refused to comply with the behaviour demanded of women, who refused to define themselves in relation to men. These women, our foresisters, millions whose names we do not know were tortured and burned as witches, slandered in religious and later in 'scientific' tracts, portrayed in art and literature as bizarre, amoral, destructive, decadent women. For a long time they represented the personification of feminine evil.

But with the emergence of feminism, lesbianism found another powerful woman-centred consciousness. For lesbian-feminists the struggle against male domination and control is no academic exercise, but a personal and political imperative. Living without the support or approval of men, lesbians desperately need women's rights. According to some[18] they are the 'front line troops' of the women's movement, engaging in the practice of which feminism is the theory, the women most harassed because they are, by definition, the most threatening to patriarchy. For heterosexual women the association of feminism with lesbianism highlights a number of contradictions. Certainly, they have been obliged to account for the potential betrayals which might occur when women who identify with women politically, still choose to have intimate relationships with men. Especially when it is appreciated that learning to love men sexually is a social process and not a natural one, and when a central feature of women's experience of male power is the control it has exercised historically over women's sexuality and fertility.

For many radical feminists the logical development of feminism is political lesbianism, but whilst separatism might be a solution at a personal level it is unlikely to provide a comprehensive solution for societal reorganisation. Not all male–female relationships are simply oppressive, but include varying degrees of mutual aid, friendship and support, and it is difficult to imagine a situation in which the majority, or even many, women would withdraw completely from relationships with men. Some will wait until reforms in the legal and social arrangements of society effect the necessary shifts in sexual relationships which make heterosexuality less compulsory and less oppressive. Others, including many lesbians, will argue for socialist rather than separatist solutions.

In the meantime, what needs to be done is to acknowledge that when women claim the right to define their own sexuality they will express their emotional and physical commitments in varied and unorthodox ways. They will not replace one orthodoxy with another, unless they repeat the patterns of patriarchy. And as with racial differences, the immediate concern for us as women is to explore and to build upon our communality of interests to avoid polarisation, and to construct a political understanding of sexuality which creates space for all of us to love whoever we choose, for the right reasons and with integrity and honesty.

Women did not create class society, but they are all products of it. Another bridge women have to make is the connection between class oppression and women's subordination to men. It is not good enough, looking from the perspective of middle-class privilege, to assume that class allegiances can be subsumed within a brave new women's culture, all-inclusive and universal in its relevance to women, whilst at the same time failing to understand that sexual oppression is a different experience if you are also working class.

Of course middle-class women are oppressed. Any woman coerced into marriage, economically dependent upon male munificence, permanently responsible for rearing children and defined primarily in relation to the success and status of the man she marries, knows about subordination. If middle-class women feel betrayed, futile, isolated, useless — their sense of failure and powerlessness is scarcely relieved by comfortable material circumstances. A split-level ranch house can be as much of a prison as a tenement flat. But the life of a working-class woman has another dimension. She is subject to constant intimidation on the basis of both sex *and* class. Chris Kent[19] describes an interview for a job in a newsagent's:

> I braced myself and knocked. 'Come in' said a voice, so I took a deep breath, coughed and went in. There sitting at the desk was, as I found out later, the Assistant Manager. 'I've come about the job' said I. 'Em' said he — talking to my tits. 'Yes' said I folding my arms. 'Yes well', he coughed, 'name etc'. The usual-type interview was conducted and then he explained that the interview was just a formality as they'd already decided who they were going to appoint. All the time he was talking to me I think he looked at my face twice. He was obviously one of those men that suffer from vertigo if they have to look higher than your bust and apoplexy if they have to look lower than your fanny. Still, he felt it would benefit us both if we had some coffee. 'Being a divorced woman' said fat gut sympathetically, 'I'm sure you must get lonely not to mention' — peels of laughter — 'frustrated'. There I sat while he continued to give me a resumé of his latest exploits, which I'm sure gave him more pleasure to talk about than to actually perform. I don't know why, but I found all of this about as interesting as the contents of a manure heap.

For women like Chris the dogma of the contemporary women's

movement is largely illusory, although she is a strong feminist and no misguided apologist for patriarchal power structures.

When Evelyn Tension joined the Women's Liberation Movement she met intellectual Marxists for the first time. 'I was amazed. *I* was who they were talking about, but I couldn't understand a word they said'. There were others — radicals — for whom class did not matter, who allowed her to talk about her life — and listened — so long as she concluded, 'We're all the same now' and 'so long as nothing (i.e. them) had to change'. For working-class women the subculture of 'professional feminism' can seem bizarre, given the very real economic stringencies of their lives and the abrasive realities of working-class machismo.

> I don't find poverty, dirt or ugliness groovy. I don't like old shirts about ten sizes too big. I don't want to look like a cross between Steptoe and a Renaissance lady. I don't really like camomile tea. I don't like fighting my way through a haze of dope, incense and Indian drapes to yet another revolutionary discussion about real true feelings.[21]

The point of discussing class is not to make middle-class women feel guilty or to caricature the women's movement. It's not to glorify being working class either. As Evelyn Tension knows, 'you don't glorify it if you've lived it'. The point is that class is basic to who we are and shapes to an enormous extent the way we see the world. The fact that we receive our social class from our fathers and our husbands makes descriptions about women based on conventional social-class categories problematic — particularly as conventional stratification models assume that women's status is equal to the status of their husbands in circumstances in which women are patently not equal to men. And yet the attitudes and values constructed within class relationships and the material conditions which circumscribe their members room to manoeuvre, mean that women living within these arrangements — which are not necessarily of their own making — are none the less profoundly affected by their implications.

Contemporary feminism must not deny these differences, romanticise them or ignore them, but recognise that different women may experience and explain oppression in different ways. Just as it is important not to describe the experience of women in different cultures according to the values of white western capitalism, so too should we appreciate how the experience of different material conditions generate different forms of oppression and different responses. There is no one simple category 'women' — either strong, brave and independent, or pitifully subservient whose social position will improve or deteriorate in the same way, and for the same reason, and at the same time, as for all other women. Class and gender relationships are more complex than this. But neither should we slip into the familiar rationalisation that some groups are better placed to endure oppression than others — the notion, for example that if a working-class woman is beaten by her husband or a prostitute is raped, that it is somehow less significant than if a 'respectable middle-class woman' becomes the victim of male violence. We should learn from history how different material conditions have generated resistance to male oppression in different ways, but ways which are linked importantly in the same pursuit of women's emancipation. Sheila Rowbotham[22] provides a good example:

19th century capital exploited poor women's labour in the factories, isolated middle-class women in the home, and forced a growing body of impecunious gentlewomen onto the labour market. Yet at the same time it brought working-class women into large scale popular movements at work and in the community, in the course of which some of them demanded their rights as a sex while resisting class oppression. Out of domestic isolation, the extreme control of middle-class men over their wives and daughters, and the impoverished dependence of unmarried women, came the first movement of feminists.

The bridges between our different material and cultural experiences are no less relevant today. Indeed, they are more urgent if we are not to repeat the mistakes of the past and miss opportunities when they occur because our visions are fragmented. This task implies an important educational dimension: we need to educate ourselves and each other. We need to learn liberation in order to be able to practise it in the full recognition that the two processes are not mutually exclusive but inextricably linked. To do this without any significant contribution from poor and black and Third World women and lesbians, is to weaken our discussion. We have the possibility to understand our differences and make them strengths, and to create a world in which we all can flourish. This, as women learning liberation, is the main purpose of our endeavour. But let us first remind ourselves what patriarchal education has done to us, and is still doing to our daughters.

Notes

1. Donna Kate Rushin, 'Bridge Poem', in Cherríe Moraga and Gloria Anzaldúa (eds) *This Bridge Called My Back: Writings by Radical Women of Color*, Persephone Press, 1981.

2. Adrienne Rich, 'Women and Honor: Some Notes on Lying', in *On Lies, Secrets and Silence: Selected prose 1966–1978*, Virago, 1980.

3. Dale Spender, *Invisible Women: the Schooling Scandal*, Writers and Readers Publishing Cooperative, 1982.

4. *Robinson Crusoe* by Daniel Defoe is generally considered, by the male-dominated literary establishment, to be the first novel. See Spender, *Invisible Women*.

5. Sheila Rowbotham, *Hidden from History*, Pluto Press, 1973.

6. Spender, *Invisible Women*.

7. Elizabeth Janeway, 'Reflections on the History of Women', in *Women: Their Changing Roles*, 1973.

8. Spender, *Invisible Women*.

9. Dorothy Smith, 'A Peculiar Eclipsing: Women's Exclusion from Man's Culture', *Women's Studies International Quarterly*, vol. 4, 1978.

10. Moraga and Anzaldúa (eds) *This Bridge Called My Back*.

11. Loraine Bethel, 'The Infinity of Conscious Pain: Zara Neale Hurston and The Black Female Literary Tradition', in Hull, Bell, Scott and Smith (eds) *But Some of Us Are Brave*, The Feminist Press, 1982.

12. Mumininas of Committee for Unified Newark, *Maranamke Mwanaychi* (the Nationalist Woman), 1971.

13. 'A Black Feminist Statement. The Combahee River Collective', in Hull *et al.* (eds) *But Some of Us Are Brave*.

14. Judit Moshkovich, 'But I Know You, American Woman', in Moraga and Anzaldúa (eds) *This Bridge Called My Back*.

15. Audre Lorde, 'The Master's Tools will Never Dismantle the Master's House', ibid.

16. Cheryl Clarke, 'Lesbianism: An Act of Resistance', ibid.

17. Adrienne Rich, 'On Lies, Secrets and Silence', in *On Lies, Secrets and Silence*.

18. Sidney Abbott and Barbara Love, *Sappho was a Right On Woman: A Liberated View of Lesbianism*, Stein & Day, 1977.

19. Chris Kent, 'Love is a Four Lettered Word', in *Words in Edgeways*, Southampton Women's Education Centre, 1980.

20. Evelyn Tension, 'You Don't Need a Degree to Read the Writing on the Wall', *Catcall* 7, 1978.

21. Tension, ibid.

22. Sheila Rowbotham, 'The Trouble with Patriarchy', *The New Statesman*, 28 December 1979.

3 THE SCHOOLING OF GIRLS

Discussions about education since the last war have queried increasingly the relationship between social class and achievement in the quest for equality of educational opportunity.[1] More recently the education system, constructed historically by the ruling class and managed by the middle class[2] to reflect the interests and requirements of dominant groups,[3] has been portrayed as an important regulator of social and economic class relations and a powerful ideological instrument[4] in the battle for the hearts and minds of dutiful workers, who need to be conformed to the rules of order required by class domination if that oppression is to be continued.

Well-known contributors to this debate in recent years have been the American historian Clarence Karier and the political economists Bowles and Gintis. They all emphasise the central importance of the economic system in society. Karier, for example, argues that through the tool of education, American schools have been used primarily to teach the attitudes and skills necessary to adjust pupils to the changing needs of the economic system, and to reinforce the values of a 'business ethic' in American society.

Bowles and Gintis develop this idea in their book *Schooling in Capitalist America*, which although argued in terms of American society, is considered highly relevant to the operation of all advanced industrial nations. According to Bowles and Gintis, the education system in society exists to produce the labour force for capitalism, both in terms of the qualities and skills needed, and also the attitudes and values likely to endorse capitalist practices. The function of education, they argue, is to anticipate and produce the conditions and the relationships which exist between employers and workers in the relationships of production. Far from being 'egalitarian' and 'reformist', as so many educators suggest, schools are about 'inequality' and 'repression'. Capitalism does not require everyone to fulfil their educational potential or become highly qualified and intellectually critical. In fact, any of these indicators of educational 'success' would, on a large scale, seriously challenge the distribution of employment, profit and power in a capitalist society. People have to be educated 'just enough' to become dutiful

29

workers, citizens and consumers, but 'not enough' to understand, or seriously challenge, the prevailing economic and social system.

The key term is 'behaviour modification' — the skills and attitudes which schools reward are diligence and obedience. And there is a 'correspondence' between the social relations of production and the social relations of education, so that children in school begin to learn the values and functions they will later repeat as workers. This is achieved, according to Bowles and Gintis, by schools modelling themselves on the hierarchical economic divisions of society, so that the relations of schooling 'replicate' the relations of production.

Bowles and Gintis do not attribute the responsibility for creating an unequal society to the education system, however; the root cause of inequality is firmly attributed to the structural divisions of capitalist society, which needs to maintain its working-class labour force. But just as capitalist society exploits the labour power of the workers, and controls so much of their social and cultural lives, so too does schooling exploit the child-workers and ensure their alienation from real learning. In different schools and in different streams, the future managers and shop-floor workers are rehearsing their future roles as organisers and organised. And all the while a façade of 'equal opportunity' and 'meritocracy' exists to confirm that educational success is alive and well, and to explain failure in terms of poor motivation and personal deficiency.

Important and influential though these arguments have been, they tend to treat the experience of girls and their preparation for domesticity and the relationships of reproduction as something that happens 'off stage'. Gender has not been taken seriously, and it is only with the re-emergence of feminism, on both sides of the Atlantic, that educational inequalities based on sex division have been identified as a major characteristic of educational systems operating under capitalist patriarchy.

Education, it is argued, is one of the many social systems created and constructed by men to sustain male power, and the notion that women might be permitted equality of opportunity within a system which men control is seen as ludicrous, given the concerns of patriarchy to present the sexual divisions of labour in society as somehow natural and inevitable.

Whilst feminist researchers[5] have contributed enormously to the dismantling of psychological and learning theories based on notions of female 'hormone deficiency' as an explanation for their

poor performance in, for example, mathematics and science subjects, the conventional wisdom that women 'are not interested' or
just 'not very good' at a whole range of educational pursuits, clings
on in the minds of those who should know better.

As Anna Coote and Beatrix Campbell[6] point out, it is all part of
the social construction of feminine psychology which is 'central to
the process of female subordination. It prepares women for their
own appointed role, and leaves them poorly qualified to perform
any of the roles that men have reserved for themselves'.

The discrediting of female ability and motivation[7] and the
circumvention of feminist criticism has a long history in a battle
which men must win if they are to pre-empt women's right to an
education system which is equally their own — an education system
in which women's experience is accepted as equally valuable and
valid as that of men, in which half the knowledge that is available is
generated by women and about women, in which women are half
the government of education, and in which women's ideas about
education are seen as equally viable and are equally implemented as
those of men.[8]

This vision of equal opportunity is far from reality, however,
although the British education system at least — allegedly open,
liberal and progressive — professes no sexist intent, and discounts
accusations to the contrary as exaggerated, irritating, tendentious
and politically misguided. So let us consider some of the evidence.

The root of the problem lies in the fact that white, middle and
upper-class men devised and fashioned an education system which
historically and contemporarily suited their purposes and reflected
their values. They created, selected, generated and confirmed with
each other, knowledge born out of their own social circumstances
and historical condition, and passed it off as a world view which
encapsulated all human experience and which has become widely
held to be objective, immutable and true.[9]

The suggestion that so-called objectivity is no more than institutionalised male subjectivity,[10] and that the knowledge which has
been produced is extremely limited by its historic lack of concern
for working-class, black and women's experience, is only now
being argued. Recent sociological debate about knowledge and
control[11] has assisted greatly in the recognition that knowledge is a
construction and transmission of selected social experience, as
distinct from fundamental and ultimate truth, but the extent to
which this is also a race-specific and patriarchal construction is

less widely appreciated.[12] It means, though, that men 'set up the system' and filled it full of knowledge and values and daily practices long before women appeared on the scene. And whilst that system may have been modified to take account of social developments and changing circumstances, and although women are now tolerated within its boundaries, its essential character has not shifted noticeably from its patriarchal origins and present patriarchal concerns.

The main struggle so far as women are concerned has been to gain access to this system. Some would claim that this battle is now largely won and 'Co-education rules OK. But those who look to co-education as the touchstone of equal opportunity and claim it as one of the greatest liberal democratic achievements of the last twenty years should consider the historical pattern, of which contemporary co-education is a development, and consider whether it actually empowers or impedes women's struggle for equality.

Jill Lavigueur's[13] summary is useful here. She reminds us that women entered the British education system in any significant numbers only in the late nineteenth and early twentieth centuries. American women made their appearance at least half a century earlier. Before the abolition of slavery most of the recruits were white, but between 1835 and 1865 nearly 140 black women attended Oberlin College, and Mary Jane Patterson became its first graduate in 1862. A good deal of the initial justification was to perfect housewifery skills however,[14] and there were plenty of those like Edward Clarke of Harvard who in 1873 argued that higher education would destroy the capacity of American women to bear children.[15]

Prejudice in Britain was similar. The general concern with eugenics and women's capacity to breed owed much to the ideas of Darwin.

It was feared that the opening of new facilities for study and intellectual improvement would result in the creation of a new race of puny, sedentary and unfeminine students, and would destroy the grace and charm of social life, and would disqualify women from their true vocation, the nurture of the coming race and the governance of well-ordered, healthy and happy homes.[16]

Pauline Marks comments,

The impression that one is left with after reading educationalists and doctors of the period, discussing topics such as the impact of education on childbirth or menstruation, is that women and girls have a fixed store of energy, a little bit of which is used up every month. If 'education' or physical exercise uses up too much of this irreplaceable store, then girls' health will be damaged with unpleasant consequences for future generations. It is fascinating to note that the way to prevent 'overstrain' is to eliminate science from the curriculum of girls' secondary schools, or at least considerably to reduce its importance.

Despite early warnings about the deleterious effects of education on women's general health and strength and their mental capacities to withstand learning, the demand for women's education increased in the middle and late nineteenth century. Although they are usually linked together in the foundation of girls' education, Dorothea Beale and Frances Buss represent, as Lavigueur makes clear, two distinct traditions. Beale, who became head of Cheltenham Ladies' College in 1858,

> developed the school in a manner which became the pattern for all girls' public schools . . . She did not seek to deviate from the Victorian feminine ideal, only to enhance it . . . [her] pupils could look forward to a leisured future and did not need to equip themselves for independence. Hence the curriculum did not neglect feminine accomplishments, and academic work, though of a far more serious nature than schools had engaged in hitherto, was of a kind thought particularly appropriate to girls.[18]

It is doubtful whether the majority of parents took the education of their daughters at Cheltenham Ladies' College altogether seriously. Most of them stayed only for a year or two, topped up with 'finishing school' abroad, on the assumption that a brief association with organised learning and training in accomplishments would be sufficient to enlighten, but not deter them from their principal ambition in life — marriage.

Frances Buss was more concerned with girls who, like herself, might be forced into providing themselves with an independent living,

The traditional structure of society outside the school was not allowed to determine the world within the school, which was firmly set to follow new directions. Social and religious distinctions were abandoned to a degree quite unusual for the age . . . academic values were put first, whilst women's traditional role was to some extent neglected (for example domestic subjects were never accorded much importance). Miss Buss set much store by the ability of her pupils to prove themselves in public examinations in open competition with boys . . . and to pursue a rigorous academic curriculum which made no concession to femininity.[19]

In the struggle for higher education Emily Davies was very much of the same mind as Frances Buss. Davies persuaded Cambridge to open its local examination to girls in 1867, and argued that women should enter university courses on the same terms as men. Although she founded Hitchen (later to become Girton College) with this in mind, and in which construction it is reported that students and professors helped to lay the bricks themselves, Cambridge did not make degrees available to women on the same terms as men until 1948. Ann Clough, head of Newnham College, on the other hand, was more concerned with improving the qualifications of women teachers, and supported the idea of special examinations for women and a different curriculum in which they would not have to compete with men.

But as a secondary and higher education was gradually extended to women, it was the Buss/Davies tradition which predominated so far as 'academic' women were concerned. The emphasis was on the similarity of intellectual needs between men and women, and was reflected in the subsequent organisation and development of girls' grammar schools. 'Intellectual accomplishments were valued more than practical ones and there was little attempt to prepare the pupils in any direct way for the role of wife and mother.'[20] Free from competition with boys in single-sex schools, girls were able to respond intellectually and emotionally in ways which assumed no sexual inferiority; they could exercise leadership and initiative and expect to inherit careers commensurate with their academic qualifications. But grammar schools catered for only a small minority of the population, and a privileged middle-class minority at that. Those present-day feminists who attribute some importance to having been educated in single-sex grammar schools[21] also regret the general exclusion of working-class girls, and comment on the painful cultural annihilation that accompanied being working class in such a school.[22]

The majority of women received their education through the tradition of elementary, secondary modern and comprehensive schools.[23] This tradition has been essentially co-educational,

> not (until recently) because of any belief in the benefits of mixed schooling, but because resources were rarely sufficient to provide separate schools . . . Within these mixed schools the two sexes were segregated as much as possible (socially and educationally) . . . so that effectively two schools existed within a common building. Within the state system, the education of boys and girls together, whenever it occurred, was purely a matter of expediency and did not imply any belief in similarity of needs.[24]

The secondary modern schools, and the comprehensives which have now virtually replaced them, adopted co-education as a practical solution to the economics of reorganisation, and ideological assumptions about separate needs continued without challenge on the understanding that boys and girls would fill distinctly different positions in society.[25] Annmarie Wolpe has carried out a close scrutiny of government reports and the wider theories of educationalists during this period and has commented upon their 'institutionalisation of the dominant female role'.[26] She found that assumptions about the future roles of girls were totally consistent with patriarchal ideologies of domesticity and femininity, and that unlike the single-sex grammar school which is based on the concern to improve the position of women, the education of the majority of girls has been within a tradition of ensuring that working class 'know their place' and that girls are taught the kinds of lessons which will confirm them in their expectation of domestic and traditional roles.

More recently co-education has been justified in other than economic terms.[27] In the late 1960s and early 1970s most liberal-progressive teachers and educationalists argued in support of co-education on the grounds that it would be 'more natural', more a reflection of 'the real world' and more consistent with ideas of equality of educational opportunity — the favourite liberal phrase — between boys and girls. Young people would be exposed to the same teachers, the same subjects and the same educational environment. In such circumstances only those who 'chose' not to avail themselves of these opportunities would be disadvantaged. Any suggestion of discrimination on grounds of sex would be finally removed.

But the problem with all of this is the assumption that *access* is the issue — access to the education traditionally monopolised by males. If the *only* education currently available is *men's* education, demanding equal access to it will not *in itself* alter the position of women and men. So long as men's definition of the world prevails and remains credited with orthodoxy, women's problems will remain the same.

If the world outside the classroom — characterised by notions of male supremacy and female subordination — is considered 'real' and 'natural', then co-education has seen to it that girls get a taste of what's to come sooner rather than later. But so far as equality of opportunity is concerned, early research findings are not encouraging. Boys are doing better at the traditional tests according to the traditional measurements,[28] girls are inhibited by the presence of boys,[29] teachers give less attention to girls[30] and mete out preferential treatment to boys at an enormous rate.[31] Boys monopolise teachers' attention[32] and talk, question and challenge more than girls.[33] 'The social structure of mixed schools may drive children to make even more sex-stereotyped choices, precisely because of the constant pressure to maintain boundaries, distinctiveness and identity',[34] and whilst science and craft facilities may be better in mixed schools, girls do not necessarily choose to have or get equal access to them.[35]

A belief in the complementary needs of the two sexes is central to the arguments supporting co-education, and the work of Roger Dale is no exception. Like all the others who have held this view, from Rousseau to Newsom, he sees women as complementing the qualities of men rather than vice versa, the feminine role being the more passive and subordinate one. His research shows that boys perform better in mixed-sex schools and girls do not perform as well, but he attributes this to the aggressiveness of the male possessing the drive needed for success, compared to the submissiveness and shyness of the female which inclines her to be 'more retiring', 'less physically active', 'less inclined to accept positions of high responsibility' and desirous of having 'as a husband a manly man to whom she can look up'.[36]

The evidence of unequal performance and conceptual prejudice notwithstanding, Dale maintains that there are considerable 'social advantages to be gained from co-education which have to be taken as seriously as those of academic performance. 'High academic attainment is not the most important aim of a school', he claims, 'we are all agreed that good character, right attitudes and healthy emotional development are of far more value'.[37] But what the social advantages to girls might be of having their academic performance depressed by the experience of co-education is not made clear.

Given these indications of concern, why have educationalists and teachers generally not made them public? Spender[38] suggests that so long as co-education is advantageous to boys, and the under-achievement of girls is not seen as a problem, the historic lack of interest of the male-dominated education system about issues concerning girls makes it unlikely that any pressure for change will come from their direction. Feminists, however, have been quick to fill the breach.

The main thrust of the feminist argument is that co-education under-pinned by patriarchal values is a system in which young women are taught their place. It is not claimed that schools and colleges do this independent of the social institutions that deal in ideological control.[39] The sexual division of labour, institution-alised within the family, has produced a unit which, depending on its economic position, not only transmits cultural capital[40] of a class character to its members, but also off-loads differing cultural values and attitudes according to whether the offspring are male or female.

The family is the social group within which children first learn their sexual identities and the behaviour which is considered to be appropriate for boys and girls. These acquisitions are considerably aided by the philosophy and strategic arrangements of the capitalist-patriarchal state, and abetted by spiritual and intellectual blockading undertaken once by religion and more recently by the media. The education system, reflective of the same interests and attitudes which characterise the wider society, does little to challenge sexism or discrimination on grounds of gender. Its main purpose is to replicate the division of labour required by capital, attune new recruits to the values required of workers, and dispense definitions of 'success' and 'failure', 'achievement' and 'incompe-tence' in ways which legitimise the propriety and apparent justice of an otherwise unequal society.

So far as girls are concerned, the responsibility of the education system is also to reinforce the logic of the sexual division of labour, and to equip young women to take their 'rightful' and 'natural' place in the sexual hierarchy. More than this, if arguments about female ineptitude and inferiority frequently advanced as the reason for their subordination are to persist, the education system has to prove men superior, whatever their social class, and encourage women to acquiesce and to internalise their own incompetence.

Virginia Woolf well understood that a principle function of women is to make men look good. 'Women have served all these centuries as looking glasses, possessing the magic and delicious power of reflecting the figure of man at twice its natural size'.[41] Dale Spender identifies the likely implications of this for girls:

It is unlikely that anyone presented with alternatives would choose the socially disadvantaged position which women occupy, and it is because they are precluded in many instances from making a choice, that education is required to make their lot more palatable. Education can assist in providing an ideological framework which justifies this disadvantage and helps make it seem reasonable. It uses propaganda to convince students that they themselves *desire* to occupy the position to which they are assigned'.[42]

There are several ways in which this is achieved. Ninety-seven per cent of the government of education is male;[43] men monopolise the positions of responsibility in schools,[44] and teach the subjects like science which are afforded most prestige. If girls are looking for role models, they will find women teachers doing more of the 'hard graft' in teaching, powerfully entrenched only in those subjects like Home Economics and Commerce which carry no prestige, and acting out their domestic and limited occupational destinies as school secretaries, dinner ladies and cleaners.

The school timetable will, since the passing of the Sex Discrimination Act in 1975, include opportunities for girls to study technical-craft subjects, but the lessons will be taught by men — and technical-studies teachers are not, on the whole, renowned for their absence of chauvinism. Priority will be given to the boys, who are considered the 'real' students when it comes to using tools and finding somewhere to work.[45] Girls will be subjected to male prejudice about their capacity to understand and handle machinery, and may — as in some schools I have visited — be confronted not unexceptionally by the pin-ups and soft porn which characteristically adorn the walls of male-determined work spaces.

It's not surprising, in these circumstances, that the majority of girls will feel unwelcome, collude in the presentation of themselves as incompetent and disinterested, and retreat to safer territory where their interests and concerns are seemingly better catered for. The terrain is deceptive, however, and the ground, though safe, is not necessarily supportive in the struggle for liberation. Since schools believe that girls' main priority is to be wives and mothers — especially non-academic, working-class and black girls — they are educated accordingly. Because 'to be different' is difficult — especially during adolescence when the pressures to conform to boys' expectations of fanciable girls is enormous — young women find themselves equipped materially and psychologically to be wives and mothers. In this way traditional domestic roles are inherited and perpetuated. By 14 or so, advice to girls about 'appropriate' subjects and 'likely' careers is largely unnecessary, because they have been well taught what to expect by their previous experience and the hidden curriculum. The penalties of being different are too costly for any but the most obstreperous or stubborn. In 'choosing' girls subjects and 'opting' for girls' careers, young women are accepting 'voluntarily' their consignment to low-status, low-paid jobs as a temporary diversion before marriage and family responsibilities consume their energies.

In times of high youth unemployment this process is likely to be exaggerated, with early marriage seen as the only viable alternative to a fruitless existence on the dole. Preparatory courses at school rarely provide the marketable skills for anything more rewarding. Women's position at the butt-end of the labour market is the successful achievement of capital's requirement for cheap, dispensible labour and patriarchy's concern for economic dependence.

In lessons which ostensibly reflect no sexual proclivities, girls still learn to know their place. Dale Spender has demonstrated how teachers mete out preferential treatment to boys at an outstanding rate.[46] Boys receive more of the teacher's attention, monopolise more of the lesson with their talk, are questioned and rewarded more, and are assumed to be brighter and more interesting to teach. Girls wait longer to have their questions answered, are rewarded only for conformity and passivity, and are treated by boys and teachers alike as less intelligent and less significant. If girls weren't in the classroom for boys to be superior to and measured against they'd have to be invented! Girls play an important part in the school construction of male superiority — they act as a negative reference group compared with whom boys can be described as superior.[47] When lessons are taped and classroom interaction is monitored, the discrepancy in the treatment of boys and girls is enormous. Usually teachers are not aware of what's happening, so accustomed are they to servicing the needs of boys first and girls second. Even those sensitive to the implications of ignoring girls are helpless to even the score when boys, sensing that they are losing the centre of the stage, 'cause trouble and get results'.[48] So long as the efficiency of teachers is judged on their demonstration of class-room control, and so long as boys have the capacity to be more noisy and troublesome than girls, then teachers will continue to appease the aggressors in the interests of peace, using a variety of strategies designed to occupy their attention and distract their capacity for disruption. Any attempt to restore the balance by focusing on the interests of girls can seem contrived and artificial, and since positive discrimination in favour of women and social intercourse which actually values the experience of women in the wider society is uncommon, it is also hard to sustain in schools. In Britain the liberal tradition, predicated on notions of individual competence, is hostile to any suggestion of 'social engineering', and teachers who argue for compensating girls by comprehensive pro-grammes of affirmative action receive little support in the average school staffroom.

Not only do most school classrooms ignore girls' experience and restrict then to roughly one third of the teachers attention,[49] but the content of lessons and the quantities of processed knowledge in school textbooks and resource kits they receive, also presents a view of the world which is man-made, and in which anything interesting, exciting, courageous, significant or creative has been done principally by men.[50] Feminist allegations about the sexism and racism of children's reading schemes has begun to have a limited impact on the character of initial reading books, and Swedish and American educational authorities have given some muscle to enlightened attempts to eliminate sex stereotyping from school text-books. But in Britain the 'professional competence' of teachers and publishers is held to be sacrosanct, and theirs is the responsibility not to teach or produce sexist material. A cursory examination of most history, geography, mathematics and science books would call into question the advisability of trusting professionals, how-ever. For many of them, their sexism is so ingrained that they do not even recognise it, and they would no doubt agree that the books are a true reflection of the way the world is, rather than the way feminists expect that it should be.

When we consider school knowledge the main concern is not with its accuracy, however, for if this were the criterion, as Spender quite pointedly observes, much of that which passes as the educational curriculum would have to be abolished; but with its contribution

> to reinforcing belief in a particular set of attitudes and values which prescribe particular places for people in society. By providing an abundance of images of positive males and a scarcity of images of females (and negative images at that) we do both sexes a disservice. We distort the humanity of both men and women. But distorted, unreal, and offensive as these images may be, they do function quite efficiently in the maintenance of a sexually unequal society

Quite simply she concludes, 'if sexism were to be removed from the curriculum, there'd be virtually nothing left to teach'.[52]

So how does the average girl respond to this experience? In 1975 Angela McRobbie[53] carried out a survey among fifty-six teenage girls who attended the same youth club, went to the same school and lived on the same council estate. As other researchers have done with boys,[54] she attempted to identify the main ways they experienced and made sen se of the world they lived in, and to consider in some detail their relationships with each other.

She began with the assumption that whatever she discovered it would be in part caused by, and certainly linked to, the social-class position of the girls, their future role in production, their present and future domestic roles and their economic dependence on their parents. She also recognised that whatever form and style the girls' culture adopted, it would be within an already established context of socially defined femininity. Needless to say, what she found was 'an ultimate if not wholesale endorsement of the traditional role of femininity, simply because to the girls this seemed to be perfectly natural'.

Since childbirth was considered to be inevitable by most of the girls, housework and child care also seemed to be unavoidable. They were the unalterable 'facts of life' which, although not always very exciting in prospect, were accepted so long as there would be friends to see them through, and so long as the 'ideology of romance' helped to compensate for reality.

The girls' leisure outlets were constrained to a large extent by their parents' earning capacity, so that for the majority of them the more expensive world of organised leisure 'up town' had to wait until they left school and were earning money of their own.

The girls were very conscious of their age and what was possible at different ages. This measuring of possibilities in terms of ages and phases is, of course, reinforced by teenage magazines which pretend that 'life goes in phases' rather than 'differences exist between classes'. (The fact that the majority of teenage magazines are implicitly directed at working-class girls is never explicitly stated in those magazines). Girls are led to expect to do different things at different ages, and each progressive phase is one step further along the inevitable female trail through dating, courtship, 'going steady' and getting wed — 'a linear career culminating in marriage'.

Age consciousness does not preclude a sense of separation from others who are different, however. The girls studied by McRobbie were working class, and she noted the extent to which common expectations and common experiences of being working class and female bound them together. Most of the girls spent between 12 and 14 hours a week in some form of domestic labour which helped their mothers, relatives or neighbours, in return for pocket money. They rarely left the estate on which they lived, they bought their clothes from the estate shopping centre or mail-order catalogues, and apart from occasional visits to relatives, their cultural space was confined to the home, the school and the youth club.

Not only were the girls' experiences limited in this way, but any other women they might meet, apart from friends and female relatives, were figures of social control — teachers, social workers, youth leaders, careers advisers and so on. Possibilities of alternative life-styles seemed, and were, remote.

School as an experience for working-class girls provided a number of contradictions. The extent to which the school continues the process of socialisation begun in the family, and is dedicated to the preparation of girls for careers in domestic labour has already been indicated, and we know from Sue Sharpe[55] and others that the ubiquity of this process is well documented. For girls who consider themselves to be failures, the culture of the school can be an alienating experience. Like 'the lads' in Willis's account of Hammertown Boys,[56] the girls in McRobbie's study had evolved strategies which enabled them to denigrate as 'snobs' and 'swots' those who were more successful than them in the school's terms. Like 'the lads' of Hammertown, many had been able to transform the school into an arena in which they could, on their own terms, develop their social life, fancy boys, learn the latest dance, have a smoke together in the lavatories, and 'play up' the teachers.

The main way chosen by the girls to oppose the mainstream culture of the school was to assert *their* own definition of femaleness, 'to introduce into the class-room their sexuality and their maturity in such a way as to force teachers to take notice'.

The definitions of femininity employed by schools are essentially middle class, and operate according to notions of 'gentleness', 'decorum', 'passivity', 'neat-and tidiness'. Working-class girls who acquire these traits, and who are separated off from 'the factory fodder' into clerical and business studies courses, will receive an expectation of upward mobility and enhanced social status as a reward. But working-class girls who retain their own cultural definitions of feminity will, so far as the school is concerned, mean trouble. The rejection of authoritarian sexism in schools (neatness, diligence, deference and passivity, for example) was achieved by the girls in McRobbie's study, by adopting an even more sexist stance of sexuality.

> Marriage, family-life fashion and beauty all contributed massively to the girls' anti-school culture, and in doing so, nicely illustrate the contradictions inherent in so-called 'oppositional' activities. Were the girls in the end, not simply doing exactly what is required of them? And if this is the case, is it not their own culture which is itself the most effective agent of social control for girls, pushing them in exactly the direction that capitalism and the whole range of institutions which support it wish them to go?

To expect working-class girls, conditioned by their class position and pressured into gender roles appropriate to their future lives as working-class housewives, to offer resistance to forces in society which have oppressed women, and working-class women in particular, for centuries is perhaps unrealistic. It is not difficult to see how the process happens, but why they continually allow it to happen, even appear to choose it, is a more complex question. Most of them realise that for them marriage is an economic necessity, and delusions about romance help them for a while to avoid facing up to the fact that the realities of marriage and child-bearing are not always quite as the magazines suggest. But whilst middle-class girls may enjoy some 'elbow room' for a few years spent at college or university, where thoughts of marriage can be at least temporarily suspended and where experiences of sexual and other relationships can be enjoyed in relative freedom for a while, there is not much place for single, working-class women in society. This is not simply a question of economics — though it will mean a life lived on the low wages of women in working-class jobs — but being forced to live as a marginal person in working-class society. Working-class girls, therefore, are doubly bound, both by the material restrictions of their class position and also by the sexual oppression of women in general.

All that this demonstrates, of course, is that those who encode the knowledge, establish the rules, determine the play and define the winners are the ones whose power can be used to further repro-duce power. It is not surprising that working-class women under-achieve and appear wrong in an education system designed and controlled by white, middle-class men, which defines success and determines excellence as essentially male qualities, and whose distinguishing characteristic is the propagation of white, middle-class men primed in turn to control and perpetuate the education system they have created and inherited Nor is it surprising that in the tradition of patriarchy and male bonding, schools dedicated to the disciplining of working-class youths in preparation for industry, will none the less endorse the superiority of boys in comparison to girls when it comes to the sexual division of labour.

We should not be surprised, therefore, that young women develop diffidence or passivity, or hostility as a response to such an experience, and emerge from it less confident about their own abilities, choosing less demanding courses, settling for lower-paid jobs, and looking to the future with a certain amount of ambivalence and resignation.

Notes

1. In, for example, A. H. Halsey, J. Floud and A. C. Anderson (eds), *Education, Economy and Society*, Free Press, 1961; R. Davie, N. Butler and H. Goldstein (eds) *From Birth to Seven*, a report of the National Child Development Study, Longman, 1972; J. W. B. Douglas, *The Home and the School*, MacGibbon & Kee, 1964; Philip Robinson, *Education and Poverty*, Methuen, 1976.

2. Doug Holly, 'The Invisible Ruling Class', in D. Holly (ed.)*Education or Domination*, Arrow (Hutchinson), 1974.

3. See, for example, Sam Bowles and Herb Gintis, *Schooling in Capitalist America*, RKP, 1976; Dale, Esland and MacDonald (eds) *Schooling and Capitalism: A Sociological Reader*, RKP, 1976; Geoff Whitty and M. F. D. Young (eds) *Society, State and Schooling*, Falmer Press, 1977.

4. Louis Althusser, 'Ideology and Ideological State Apparatuses; Notes Towards an Investigation', in *Lenin and other essays*, New Left Books, 1971.

5. See, for example, C. S. Dureck and Coetz, 'Attributions and Learned Helplessness', *New Directions in Attribution Research*, vol. 2, Halstead, 1978; C. S. Dureck, 'Learned Helplessness and Legative Evaluation', *Education*, vol. 19, (2); E. Fennema, 'Influences of Selected Cognitive, Affective and Educational Variables on Sex Related Differences in Mathematics, Learning and Studying', *Women and Mathematics: Research Perspectives for Change*, NIE Papers in Education and Work, no. 8, 1977; E. Fennema and J. Sherman, 'Sex Related Differences in Mathematics Achievement and Related Factors: A Further Study', *Journal for Research in Mathematics Education*, no. 9, 1978; E. Maccolsy and C. Jacklin, *The Psychology of Sex Differences*, Stanford University Press, 1974; Alison Kelly (ed.) *The Missing Half*, Manchester University Press, 1981.

6. Anna Coote and Beatrix Campbell, *Sweet Freedom*, Picador, 1982.

7. Pauline Marks, 'Femininity in the Classroom: An Account of Changing Attitudes', in Juliet Mitchell and Ann Oakley (eds) *The Rights and Wrongs of Women*, Pelican, 1976.

8. Dale Spender, *Invisible Women: The Schooling Scandal*, Writers' and Readers' Publishing Cooperative, 1982.

9. Dorothy Smith, 'A Peculiar Eclipsing: Women's Exclusion from Man's Culture', *Women's Studies International Quarterly*, vol. 1, no. 4.

10. Adrienne Rich, *On Lies, Secrets and Silence*, Virago, 1980.

11. Michael F. D. Young (ed.) *Knowledge and Control*, Collier–Macmillan, 1971.

12. Spender, *Invisible Women*.

13. Jill Lavigueur, 'Co-education and the Tradition of Separate Needs', in D. Spender and Elizabeth Sarah (eds) *Learning to Lose*, The Women's Press, 1980.

14. Phyllis Stock, *Better than Rubies: A History of Women's Education*, Capricorn Books, 1978.

15. Ibid.

16. J. Fitch, 'Women and the Universities', *Contemporary Review*, August 1980.

17. Pauline Marks, 'Femininity in the Classroom'.

18. Lavigueur, 'Co-education and the Tradition of Separate Needs'.

19. Ibid.

20. Ibid.

21. 'Girls' Schools Remembered', *Women and Education*, vol. 13, 1978.

22. Irene Payne, 'A Working-class Girl in a Grammar School', in Spender and Sarah (eds) *Learning to Lose*.

23. Brian Simon and David Rubinstein, *The Evolution of the Comprehensive School*, RKP, 1973.

24. Lavigueur, 'Co-education and the Tradition of Separate Needs'.

25. See, for example, *The Crowther Report*, 1959 and *The Newsom Report*, 1963, HMSO.

26. Annemarie Wolpe, *Some Processes in Sexist Education*, Women's Research and Resources Centre, 1977.

27. Roger R. Dale, *Mixed or Single Sex Schools?*, in three volumes, RKP, 1969, 1971, 1974.

28. Eileen Byrne, *Women and Education*, Tavistock, 1978.

29. Sue Sharpe, *Just Like a Girl*, Penguin, 1976; Florence Howe, 'The Education

of Women', in Stacey *et al.* (eds) *And Jill Came Tumbling After'*, Dell, 1974.

30. Pauline Sears and David Feldman, 'Teacher Interaction with Boys and Girls', in Stacey *et al.* (eds) *And Jill Came Tumbling After.*

31. Spender, *Invisible Women.*

32. Ibid.

33. Ibid; and Angela Parker, 'Sex Differences in Classroom Intellectual Argumentation', unpublished MSc. thesis, Pennsylvania State University, 1973.

34. Jenny Shaw, 'Sexual Divisions in the Classroom', paper presented at conference, 'Teaching Girls to be Women', Essex, 1977.

35. Byrne, *Women and Education.*

36. Roger Dale, 'Education and Sex Roles', *Educational Review*, vol. XXII, no. 3, 1975.

37. Ibid.

38. Spender, *Invisible Women.*

39. Althusser, 'Ideology and Ideological State Apparatuses'.

40. Pierre Bourdieu, 'Cultural Reproduction and Social Reproduction', in R. Brown (ed.) *Knowledge, Education and Cultural Change*, Tavistock, 1974.

41. Virginia Woolf, *A Room of One's Own*, Penguin, 1974.

42. Dale Spender, 'Education or Indoctrination', in Spender and Sarah (eds) *Learning To Lose.*

43. Byrne, *Women and Education.*

44. Ibid.

45. Spender, *Invisible Women.*

46. Ibid.

47. Ibid.

48. Ibid.

49. Ibid.

50. Marian Scott, 'Teach Her a Lesson: Sexist Curriculum in Patriarchal Education', in Spender and Sarah (eds) *Learning to Lose.*

51. Spender, 'Education or Indoctrination', *Invisible Women.*

52. Ibid.

53. Angela McRobbie, 'Working-class Girls and the Culture of Femininity', in *Women Take Issue*, Hutchinson, 1978.

54. Paul Willis, *Learning to Labour: How Working-class Kids get Working-class Jobs*, Saxon House, 1979.

55. Sharpe, *Just Like a Girl.*

56. Willis, *Learning to Labour.*

4 THE PERSONAL IMPLICATION OF WOMEN'S SUBORDINATION

PRISONERS

Every street, road, village, town has them,
Small dots at windows.
Watching, waiting patiently
For escape, a chance to be free,
Hours turning to days, to weeks,
to months and years.
Lives are wasting,
like stale vegetation.
Chained by guilt,
unable to be free
Somebody must help them
before their lives end.

Too late,
More lives lost.

Angela Weaver[1]

Single status in a culture in which marriage is encouraged is not the only form of marginality that women can expect to experience. Although women in Britain actually outnumber men in the population,[2] the sense of being as equally as important as men in the organisation and deliberations of the state is not part of women's experience. The history of human endeavour, the concerns of *men* and the future of *man*kind are all concepts which we assume embrace women within their frame of reference, but in the process of constructing a grammar which neatly subsumes she within he, and her within him, we have lost sight not only of feminine symbols, but also of female reality and experience.

Elaine Morgan[3] is absolutely right when she says that the prehistory of mankind would reflect very different assumptions about the world if we were to find recorded that 'When the first ancestor of the human race descended from the trees she had not yet developed the mighty brain that was to distinguish her so sharply from other species'.

47

It is not merely that the English language reflects male experience and male constructs,[4] or that the mediation of expertise and the formulation of opinions are controlled and delivered by men,[5] but that shared social conditions like work and unemployment, sport and recreation, political activism and unrest all appear as male issues and male concerns.

Somewhere in the presentation of male reality and male perspectives as the totality of human experience, women have ceased to exist in a serious and visible way. Women have become marginal to the general concerns of human existence, which is in fact male existence. Women appear only in sex-specific discussions about, for example, mating and mothering and making ends meet. In matters of general concern the voice of authority is male, and Joe Public is exactly who his masculine name suggests. An important lesson we need to learn as women is to discover how power in the hands of men has been used to determine our marginality, and why we have accepted this position. The words of women included here are of course their own, but they carry with them the collective wisdom of countless women who have lived and shared a similar experience.

As we have seen, the concern of schooling is to teach women a salutary lesson — to know their place and to accept it. For many, school has been a meaningless and unpleasant experience in which it was usual to feel marginal, although not always to understand why.

As for schooldays — I don't really remember much about them. I know the secondary modern was vast with hundreds of kids all around. I didn't like it from the start. The teachers didn't seem to care whether you understood what they said. Things were pumped into you — if they stayed in your brain, all well and good, if they didn't, too bad. I never had the courage to question and so I just plodded on and left at 15 — not very bright but not quite a twit. I just hated it all.

I suppose I would be classed as one of the millions of failures. Maybe half of it was my fault. I suppose you would call me a non-conformist. I found it difficult to comply with all those petty rules and regulations and consequently alienated myself from the teachers. They had labelled me as a troublesome pupil. There was no point in working because I knew I couldn't stay on to take exams (I came from a large family and the need to earn a wage was ever present) and I feel that any effort on my part would be wasted anyway. The teaching itself was on the whole uninteresting and boring. There never seemed to be much effort put into the actual enjoyment level of the pupils. The teachers kept themselves apart — they stood at the front of the class and talked 'at' us rather than 'to' us . . . On the whole it was all too formal. The overall feeling was that they were there because it was their job, and we were there because the law stated that we had to be. I left at the age of 15 with no qualifications, labelled by the teachers as 'factory fodder'. In this respect I did conform to their expectations — I became exactly what they said.

Some teachers were so boring, so indifferent. They would just walk into the class, try and get some order, tell you what page of the book to work from and then sit out the lesson. Some almost seemed to begrudge answering questions. One guy always sat there picking his nose and flicking it. You didn't learn much geography, but by God your reflexes were good!

After a period of low-paid, unskilled employment and then marriage, many women awake to a fairly frightening reality and sense of confusion.

Living on an estate has shown me the feeling of hopelessness that so many working-class women feel. Trapped by bad education, early marriage and children. The situation of women who never get together to talk unless it's about kids or 'the prices'. The feeling that to want something else or more is odd. I am aware of my ignorance but I have an instinctive feeling about the injustice of the educational system that turned me loose on the streets at 15 yrs. old knowing all about 1066 and how to make a Christmas cake with the expectation of working for two or three years. Then marriage. Then kids. That was success. That was what I had been raised for. Well I have found it all a con game. It's not enough for me. I need more but I don't know where to start.

I feel very frustrated and sometimes (actually nearly all the time) very angry at many things happening in our world today, and more so because I don't feel a part of what is going on. I would like to contribute something in some way, but I don't know where or how to begin.

When I left school I had no qualifications and the types of work open to me were very limited. There I was — knowing that I wanted to do something, but lacking the knowledge or the confidence to do anything about it. I felt I had a lot to give. I wanted to do a worthwhile job. But there were no openings — no-one to show the way. It was really very frustrating. I became more and more dissatisfied with my own life. I must have been hell to live with. The dissatisfaction was not a new feeling, I had felt it on and off for several years but could never actually put a finger on the reason for it — just the constant thought that there must be more to life than this.

Back to Betty Friedan's 'problem with no name',[6] the sites and situations different, but the hopelessness of marginality exactly the same. Others recognise their supposed good fortune — a nice home, a decent husband, two lively children — but still the insignificance and isolation which can, and frequently does, lead to loneliness, futility and despair.

I always thought that when people overdose they just calmly fall asleep and that is the end of that. But I didn't, the aspirins blew the top off my head and I was wide awake, fully aware of everything, yet resigned to the fact that what I'd done, I had wanted to do, because I couldn't find, in all those years, a way of escaping the misery I felt. I felt guilty at my inability to cope in situations which only got worse. The frustration of standing at the stove being totally unable to cook a meal. The lack of concentration when shopping — grabbing everything just to get away from the place, trembling hands as I stood in a queue which seemed to have stopped dead. Visiting a friend and as soon as I arrived wanting to leave. Sitting for hours on the bedroom floor staring into space, not answering the door or phone because I felt so withdrawn. The effort of making myself drive when I'd lost my confidence. But in reverse, pacing about like a penned-in tiger feeling I would blow up any minute if I didn't get out of the house. Floods of tears, feeling helpless yet frustrated.

The medical solution? — pills, psychotherapy and hospitalisation. Looked at with compassion, the idea of medication and behaviour-modification intended to adjust women to the acceptance of unsatisfactory circumstances seems a brutal and insensitive reaction to declarations of inadequacy and despair. But marginality is not a part of the general experience of men, and remains unnamed as a problem within their experience. Certainly, if it were, and if men shared on the same scale the futility and isolation of women's lives, which reduces countless thousands to mental breakdown and dependency on drugs, reactions would be very different. The problem would be named, it would become a national scandal, a cause for concern and a target for immediate government action. So long as men do not experience it, however, it is as though the problem doesn't exist.

The search for understanding and knowledge to deal with feelings of frustration and exclusion has led others up scarcely more illuminating blind alleys — towards more education, sex and politics.

I didn't always feel very confident — quite the reverse most of the time, but because I was reasonably bright (and it was the early 60s, remember), I felt fairly optimistic about my own chances. I had the sense that 'my thing could happen' — that there must be so much out there — beyond the narrow confines of that bourgeois, anti-ideas, stultifying atmosphere I grew up in — that I could reach out to a 'body of knowledge' and make it my own — find my own oasis and deliverance from feelings of marginality. And so I did reach out — but 'the knowledge' was all male and the experience wasn't mine — it was all Sartre, Camus, Colin Wilson, Kerouac, even Nietzche if you were really into impressing — but I never knew 'til later why I felt wrong — crazy really, when it all seems so obvious now.

The kind of liberation we were being pushed into was sexual liberation. I remember feeling under great sexual pressure and feeling guilty-prudish — if I didn't want to screw — like I was suffering from false sexual consciousness which had to be overcome by correct thinking and practice. And how we could get abortions pre-67, and afterwards finding a 'friendly' GP who would give us the pill — he did, but we had to put up with him shoving his fingers up us, and when we protested, him making obscene comments about what did we want the pill for, then, if we didn't want to be stuffed? And having to put up with it because we needed the pill and he was the only one around who would give it to us. Of course we know now it was all a con, we were being used yet again. Sexual liberation was merely about removing even more of the barriers that prevented us being readily available to men.

When I joined the Campaign Against Racial Discrimination I didn't realise how easy it is to get involved in other people's oppression for the wrong reasons — and it's not to invalidate the process or to deny the anger I felt about it — and still do — but the effect upon one's feelings of marginality — double marginality actually — are enormous. You're 'outside' because you can't concur with the views of mainstream society, and marginal because, by not being black, your role (other than the one prescribed by Stokely Carmichael) is really minimal if you are sensitive to the real issues. It was as if I was so used to feeling for other people, carrying guilt, all those things, that I never stopped to feel for myself. It seems like I've been carrying it all around for a long time now, and whilst my anger about racism has not diminished — my anger about my early blindness to my own position has increased.

Every woman has a well-stocked arsenal of anger, frequently stifled, sometimes turned against herself, but potentially useful against the oppressions, both personal and institutional, which brings that anger into being. In some circumstances it's called guts.

My husband is an alcoholic and after many years of struggle I plucked up courage and got a legal separation. So there I was — a single parent living on a council estate, responsible for six kids and of course no maintenance. It took all of this for me to realise how deeply disadvantaged working class families living on low incomes really are.

I glibly stated we were hard up — hard up in my mind was temporary — not poor, poor being an attitude of mind in which hope had died and apathy reigned eternal. The school holidays were the worst. We couldn't afford outings or holidays. So I started looking around for some way of compensating. Me and my kids and others who cared to come along walked many miles that first year — to the sports centre, to the common, to the pier — anywhere we didn't have to pay. One day I had fifteen kids with me.

About this time Southampton Children's Play Association got

off the ground and I became involved, working voluntarily with kids in the school holidays. At first it was very exciting, surely this was the beginning of community action, an activity which the local community would gather round and begin to take stock of their situation and really work to cause some improvement. They would begin to realise that they lived in sub-standard houses, that they had virtually no choice in where they lived or what schools their children were to attend. But none of this happened. I became involved with several other community projects. Always the leaders of these projects were professional people acting out their social consciences in some project that was fashionable at that particular time. Usually up to a point they were successful but always always always they would stick it for a couple of years and when the going got tough they would move onto something more fashionable or lucrative.

What all this is leading up to is my feeling of powerlessness — that unless I can produce evidence of my success i.e. commercial, academic or marriage, my opinions will never be considered credible.

Feelings of marginality, powerlessness, isolation and guilt frequently conspire to defuse in women the creative energy of anger.

I remember my lonely anger at issues that arose in my own town, at school, at university where women and girls were so outrageously discriminated against and exploited. The first Abortion Law Reform Act in the late sixties stands out as a monument to the prevailing arrogant attitudes of men who saw themselves as unquestionably able and responsible for debating and legislating on issues that fundamentally were the concern of women. I felt shame and humiliation at that time both personally and on behalf of women everywhere — but guilt too because there was no-one with whom to share these emotions, no-one who could validate me by offering the strength of a similar perception.

Others of us, as women, are agents of our own oppression — until the contradictions become unbearable.

But I, just as much as the males who dominated and legislated for my life's comfort and well-being, was a prisoner of history and culture. To a very large extent I too accepted the *status quo* as the natural order of things. For all the earlier years of marriage when the children were small, I simply took it for granted that the wife was the home-maker and the husband was the wage-earner, and I took on without question, indeed happily, many of the consequences of this division. There were some things though that I did query but I was made to feel very guilty and ungrateful about these. I felt there was something wrong in the reality that the person who was the wage-earner, was also, almost by that fact, the main decision maker; that the wage-earners time was seen as more valuable, and his opinions better informed and of greater insight that the home-makers; that his outside commitments, however many hours they occupied, were almost always awarded first priority. These sorts of issues — some of them important others less so — that could never be openly talked about because the climate did not allow it, or because they were trivialised, eventually became the focus (still sometimes unspoken) of increasing resentment and recrimination. Much more was added as new attitudes and my own widening experience brought the realisation that these guilt-ridden doubts and longings were not after all just the petulant, self-indulgent demands of the discontented child, but the necessary foundations for the wholesome, even though belated growth of the adult self.

Growth through anger, focused with precision, can be a powerful source of energy, serving progress and change. Anger expressed and translated into actions in the service of women's visions and women's futures can be a liberating and strengthening act of clarification, for it is in the painful process of this translation, that we identify who are our genuine allies and who are our enemies.

For many years he made light of what I did and I endured my frustration in private. When I became depressed he got heated and said other women were content why couldn't I be. He said it was my duty to think of the children and put the family first. I did love the children and they were my salvation in a way but I found it hard to keep loving him. In fact I felt responsible for him and guilty — always guilty — but didn't often think in terms of love anymore. I used to have secret dreams of getting on a plane somewhere — anywhere — I didn't care — but having the chance to start again. It was all pipe dreams of course. So long as I put up with it all, and made sure everyone else was happy, it was alright. When I thought I'd go insane and started to look outside and find a life for myself he became more obstinate. He began to trivialise my new interests in education and make sarcastic remarks about my friends. I suppose he felt jealous and threatened. He wouldn't look after the children so that I could go out, although he went out all the time just as he pleased. He even reduced the housekeeping money because he said I was spending too much of it on myself. When he hit me all the guilt turned to anger — anger that I had denied my real feelings for so long, anger that the circumstances in which I lived and which I never divulged to any other human being nearly cracked me up, and anger that anyone — especially my husband — could use his physical strength against me in that way and do what he did. In another way though, it made it easier. I lost my guilt and any respect I might have had for him. It makes the decision to get a divorce easier and now there's no turning back.

For others there are lapses of momentum, however, because to see clearly the issues women have to confront needs the strength to renounce the strategies we use to bind ourselves by our guilt and blind ourselves to the real implications of change.

I always felt capable of doing something other than translating someone else's shorthand into legible English but I don't know what. I don't have any qualifications for anything. I feel very much like the mere appendage of my family. I'm Paul's wife — Tony and Emma's mother. As my children grow I become less important to their existence — providing clean clothes and hot meals — I have to find something more personally fulfilling. I am frustrated by my inability to do anything well, also worried as I know that whatever confidence I did possess has been swallowed up somewhere between nappies and decorating. I want to break out — but feel guilty for wanting something different. My family seems to constantly expand their lives and I seem to shrink in amongst them.

My own efforts to work out the contradictions and feelings of frustration within marriage failed. My husband left, but the

losses that I felt in accompaniment with his departure and afterwards were almost overwhelming — for although I deeply
believed in the issues I had been pursuing I had not been working
from a position of inner strength or personal autonomy. Far
from it; I was in fact still involved in, and even dependent on,
some of the very supports which in the end had felt like the bars
of a restraining cage. Without them I was lost and frightened,
totally self-doubting, hopelessly uncertain as to which new
direction was the one to take.

For many women the feeling of having little confidence is widespread — it represents anxieties which are rarely expressed by men
in quite the same way. The feelings are almost always attributed to
some sense of personal inadequacy and are strongest when women,
used to being home-makers and child-rearers, venture 'out' into the
world beyond the home. Many of us underrate our own strengths
and achievements, and after a number of years in which our lives
have revolved around the needs of our husbands and children, we
lose track of our own identity and sense of significance. And yet to
collude with this assessment of self-depreciation is to miss several
salient points, not least of which is the extent to which self-
confidence is in fact a measure of essentially male experience.
Women who are educated and qualified, or who do a job that
entitles them to wages, or who experience some involvement in
public (as distinct from domestic) life — in short, women who are
regarded as people in their own right rather than 'merely' someone's wife or someone's mother — are much less likely to feel
unconfident than women whose relationships with the outside
world are mediated through their relationships with husband and
children, and who are defined principally in terms of these relationships. No women of course, however educationally qualified,
career-minded or publicly committed, can automatically withstand
the destruction of self-confidence that can accompany domesticity.

To suddenly find myself responsible for a child and then a
second and a third, from an area where I had a job I liked and
friends, to be out of control of my own life — only then did I
really feel it in my guts that this was it, this was what it was all
about, this is what it is that keeps us in our place. Children aren't
a shared responsibility — they're *our* responsibility. And
although I knew in my head that it wasn't fair and things should

be different the experience of it all still had the effect of making me feel useless within a matter of months.

What is being defined as lack of confidence, then, is most frequently the lack of opportunity, the absence from, or the lack of experience of participating in social interaction outside the home which is not predetermined by domestic responsibilities and relationships. In other words, the reality of experiencing a male-centred world as women rather than as men, and blaming ourselves for feeling unconfident about doing those things from which we have been generally excluded.

If the status and significance of the two worlds — public and domestic — were reversed, and the domestic was credited with supreme importance, the majority of men might equally be found lacking in confidence, because their experience would be largely irrelevant and the qualities they had acquired from their socialisation would be seen as less valuable and less appropriate. Women who claim to be unconfident are in most respects internalising and taking responsibility for a process of exclusion and marginalisation which is a consequence of patriarchal relationships. Their acceptance represents a classic example of victimisation and victim-blaming rather than the recognition of structural oppression.

Their acceptance is also ironic because the work women undertake at home, the domestic servicing of men and children, the care-taking, and the emotional management of family life at whose centre is the mother, and whose labour and fortitude historically have served to keep families together through often trying and difficult times, represent the kinds of skills and self-sacrifice and resilience which, if they were men's skills and men's work, would be enormously regarded and rewarded.

It seems outrageous that we have allowed any women who takes on these responsibilities happily, or who endures them with resignation as a fact of life, or who releases herself from them in disenchantment or despair, to feel that she is incapable of anything else. To revalue women's domestic labour and its contribution to the general well-being of others is therefore important — although caring in this way should not be used as a justification for their subordination in society. Women's place is anywhere they want to be in the world, and whilst this might include the home it also, and increasingly, might not. Neither is this to suggest that all women's experience of family life is painful and unhappy. Clearly it is not.

But family happiness should not preclude alternative and additional fulfilments — it should enhance them. A woman should not have to choose between the enrichment and development of her own true self and the demands made upon her by her family. But very frequently this is exactly what happens. She denies her own growth in the development of theirs and if, for any reason, things go wrong with those relationships she is left in a more vulnerable position than she would otherwise have been.

The discrepancies between the prevailing view that women should find fulfilment in their families, and the dissatisfactions which confuse, anger and depress so many women, have to be taken seriously. And as increasing numbers of women find themselves, or choose to be, on the outside of conventional two-parent family arrangements, the discrepancy between the myth and the reality intensifies. Feelings of marginality, frustration, lack of confidence, personal anonymity and depression are too common among too many women in too many different economic and social circumstances to be dismissed as the disabilities and deficiences of an ungrateful few. Neither is it helpful to have such feelings — different in degree and intensity among different women — diagnosed as hormonal or the emotional consequences of female biology. The root causes are social and are a compliment to the subordination of women in a society in which men hold, and have held historically, personal and public power. So long as men continue to excerise superordinate control — however gentle, protective, and chivalrous it may seem — women will be encouraged and expected to accept their role in the male scheme of things willingly or dutifully.

Confronted alone, the implications of frustration, anger and change are all too easily doubted and denied, but once women begin to check their experience with each other and begin to name the feelings honestly which get in the way of growth and autonomy, the way is progressively cleared for the creation of very different possibilities. And in this process there is none more competent than another. There are no 'teachers' and no 'learners' — every women's truth is equally important, as this account makes clear:

> I joined a women's group after the break-up of my marriage which had lasted twenty years. I faced the future with total fear but wanted to feel positive. Early meetings were amazingly different experiences but they shared common features. Firstly was the warmth of acceptance — no passport other than the fact

of being a woman was needed — all the usual barriers of age, class, marital status, educational achievement, career or lack of it — were irrelevant. . . We were women and it was understood that there was a shared history and a common experience that could hold us together. From this came a freedom in conversation that was entirely new to me and almost intoxicating in its freshness. Everything was of interest and we were all eager to listen rather than compete for the next cue to offer our own next statement. All the time there was encouragement and validation. I found that so much of my own experience was shared and understood by others. It became clear that so many matters that I had previously felt guilt and shame about were not shameful or morally reprehensible at all — that some of my desires and aspirations were legitimate — and more than that, achievable. I felt strength begin to flow; there was the possibility that the fragmented self could begin to heal and grow again.

All the women that I know in the movement are involved in an adventure. We do things which in previous times of our life we would have never thought possible. We dance and make jokes and wear badges that make statements about ourselves that we would never have dared to be let known before. Some women bravely re-start formal education which previously had been halted abruptly in adolescence, others experiment with art or writing or making radio programmes — anything at all, somebody will try. And it is all possible because fundamentally we say 'yes, we know we have potential; we know that each and every one of us has untapped areas of talents that society, or we ourselves in the condition in which we live, have not been able to fulfil'. We respect each other in whatever we try to do. We don't compete or put down — we combine when that will be fruitful, and give or receive encouragement for whatever we have to do alone.

It is early days for me and I have the dilemma of whether, how and when to try and reconcile people from other phases of my life. But what I think is new for me and the others, is that change is happening more rapidly and on many fronts than ever before and we have not just an opportunity but a responsibility, both collectively and personally, to make some statement about it. We may be unsure because for some the opportunity may have been almost forced upon us, and may still be in battle with old attitudes. But I think our responsibility is not to let the wool come down over our eyes again, is to hold to the new awareness that we have gained, and is to stay confident in, and use wherever we can, the strengths that we have gained from our discovery of each other.

Women who join women's groups or who have found with other women understanding and answers that make sense, have not done so out of a general satisfaction with the *status quo*, but from the conscious conviction that as women they are entitled to a fairer, more just and qualitatively richer life. The reconstruction of our world means that the relationships between men and women will have to change if both are not to be dehumanised or destroyed.

In this process of change education both formal and informal has an important part to play. The development of skills to analyse our situation and our condition wisely, the opportunity to learn from the experience of others, and the encouragement to practise our expectation of new possibilities are an essential accompaniment to the material and spiritual independence of women. But the education that will assist women in this quest will also have to be of our own making if it is to take account of our reality and our needs for, as we shall see, that which is, and that which has been provided for us by men is an unreliable ally in the struggle for liberation.

Notes

1. Angela Weaver, 'Prisoners', in *On Second Thoughts*, Southampton Women's Education Centre, 1981.

2. UK Population 1979: men 27.3 million; women 28.7 million (official government statistics).

3. Elaine Morgan, *The Descent of Woman*, Souvenir Press, 1972.

4. Dale Spender, *Man Made Language*, RKP, 1980.

5. Anna Coote and Beatrix Campbell, *Sweet Freedom*, Picador, 1982.

6. See page 9.

5 ADULT EDUCATION — THE HISTORICAL CONSTRUCTION OF PATRIARCHAL ATTITUDES

The promise of education is of knowledge and understanding which will enrich life, and of qualifications which will sweep individuals out of drudgery and meaningless employment into well-paid and satisfying careers. The rhetoric is very far from the reality for the majority of school-leavers, however. Unemployment among young people under twenty-five is increasing dramatically throughout Europe and North America, and the correlation between decent jobs and qualifications is not nearly so clear cut as it once was. In these circumstances discussions about 'recurrent education', 'continuing education' and 'lifelong learning' seem to make more sense in a world in which the future is less predictable than it seemed to the policy pundits of an earlier generation. And as adult education is charged with new significance, it is interesting to consider its past record and present possibilities so far as women are concerned.

Feminist analysis of education has tended to concentrate on the period of formal schooling and, as we have seen, presents a fairly gloomy picture so far as young women are concerned. The career of girls through the education system is characterised by a progressive deterioration in their levels of attainment, and any parity maintained with boys in early adolescence soon dissipates beneath the surge of sexist pressures endemic in the assumptions of patriarchal education and commercial youth cults. As Annmarie Wolpe concludes, 'This deterioration appears as a rejection by adolescent girls, a total rejection of school culture, and most forms of studying, they opt rather for whatever job is available and for early marriage'.[1] So far the analysis has concentrated on schooling. Most adult educationalists would argue that their practices are not equivalent to those of the school and as such do not merit the same kind of scrutiny. Women are well represented among their students, although working-class adults are conspicuous by their absence.[2]

The first thing to notice is that what is commomly referred to as 'adult education' is, in fact, only a small part of the post-school education available to adults. In terms of its relation to qualifications, its links with powerful academic interests and its ability to control and make available the knowledge required by prestigious elites, its contribution is marginal.

The provision of post-graduate studies and the organisation and control of research by the universities is not regarded as 'adult education'. Similarly, the array of professional qualifications available to lawyers, doctors, accountants and business managers, for example, all imply specialist and advanced study in keeping with the status and decision-making authority of present and future elites. But none of this comes under the conventional definition of adult education. Polytechnics, and the existence of specialist colleges of art, drama and music provide yet another example. If it is true that the education system reflects in its subdivisions the hierarchical nature of the wider society, it is undoubtedly the case that the kind of education for adults usually referred to as 'higher education' is where the influence and power lie. In terms of the educational pecking order, the adult education we know — that which is provided by university extramural departments, the Workers' Educational Association (WEA) and local education authorities (LEAs) — is small scale and second rate in comparison. Its low position in the hierarchy is in direct relation to its minimal contribution to conferring qualifications upon, and confirming the status of, signicant social elites. In fact, as Enid and Edward Hutchinson point out, it is 'dominated by concepts of leisure-time satisfaction'[3] and intrinsically valuable though these might be, they have low currency value in a meritocratic education system servicing a work-orientated society.

It would be wrong to suggest that adult education is the 'poor cousin' which serves the interest of the poor, however. Its relationship to the institution of higher education might seem analogous to the secondary modern's relationship to the grammar school, in terms of resources, prestige and influence, but there the analogy stops. Any suggestion that adult education is an alternative means of educational provision for the less educated is very far from true. In many ways it exists as a microcosm of the wider educational system, with the same inbuilt sense of hierarchy operating to consolidate the educational and social divisions pre-empted by schooling in a capitalist society.

The fact that in the main the products of adult education are consumed by a small and socially discreet section of the population, is well documented.[4] They attract those members of the middle and lower middle class who have already experienced a fair amount of 'educational success', who consider 'organised learning' to be a valuable and interesting endeavour, and who are not principally motivated by vocational considerations. The ideal of 'education for its own sake' is one which the university tradition in adult education has deliberately cultivated. Its roots in academic scholarship and the patronage of the leisured and genteel classes in the nineteenth century[5] have contributed to the sense of detachment from contemporary society. Current defenders of this tradition still advocate it in preference to the 'practical instrumentalism' which they associate with more recent innovations like trade union studies and community education.[6] In the same tradition the contributors to the Russell Report (1973) claim that,

> the value of adult education is not solely to be measured by direct increases in earning power or productive capacity, or by any other materialist yardstick, but by the quality of life it inspires in the individual and generates in the community at large.[7]

Another characteristic of adult education is the demarcation between providers, both in what they offer and in whom they attract. In general terms, the university extramural tradition has grown out of intramural degree courses and the dissemination of academic knowledge in a manner associated with scholarship and sustained study. The WEA provision has, in many respects, become barely distinguishable from that promoted by the universities, despite its roots in workers' education and political and economic studies.[8] As a consequence, its students reflect the same social class and 'degree of schooling' as those who attend extramural classes, though it is generally claimed that WEA level work provides only an introduction to the academic humanities. Students who wish to deepen their understanding of the subject being studied would need the guidance of a university-appointed tutor.[9]

LEAs, on the other hand, provide educational activities which are more concerned with 'practical', 'recreational' and 'creative' subjects, rather than 'academic studies', thus continuing the demarcation between high-status and low-status knowledge so familiar in the school curriculum.[10] LEA provision does not, on the whole, lead to any kind of advanced qualifications, and is more closely identified with hobbies and leisure-time pursuits than the courses provided by the universities and the WEA. Whilst it might be expected that the provision of a fairly comprehensive range of offerings, depending on the size and status of the centre, could be expected to appeal to a cross-section of the population, the social composition of LEA adult-education classes is only slightly different from that of the universities and the WEA. LEA students tend to be slightly older than responsible-body students, and lower middle-class as distinct from middle class in social standing. Women outnumber men by about three to one.[11]

Women also outnumber men in university and WEA provision by roughly two to one — in fact non-vocational adult and further education is the only sector of the education system in which women constitute a majority interest.

A good deal of the provision associated with 'disadvantaged' groups — especially English as a second language for immigrants, literacy, adult basic education schemes and community education — rely on voluntary labour. The principle of retaining most resources and the most favourable teaching-learning conditions for those who have already had most out of the education sysytem remains prevalent, and softened by a philosophy of virtuous thrift to explain away the rest.

Women, are both visible and invisible in adult education. They have consistently supported adult-education activities in large numbers, and yet the practices and ideologies that combine to make adult education what it is do not make this apparent.[12] At times the support of women has been recognised, but only in specific ways. In general, adult education has been slow to respond to the concern of its participants, and has continued to reinforce traditional assumptions which mitigate against women's progress towards equality. This is most clearly evident in the curriculum of the LEAs, as we shall see, but is none the less true in the selection and transmission of cultural values and knowledge which characterises university and WEA provision.

A cursory examination of university and WEA programmes displays a similar consensus in terms of what it is thought appropriate to offer as the core curriculum identified by Wiltshire and Mee[13] in their survey of LEA adult education. This extract from the Southampton University programme for 1980–1 is fairly typical of others, and displays the usual commitment to the social and cultural values of dominant groups, and to the dissemination of male-centred knowledge constructed, written and promoted by an academic tradition which has credited high status to its own concerns.

The Physical Landscape of the New Forest
The Philosophy of Man
Poetry Now
The Pre-History of Hampshire — Neolithic to the Iron Age
La Langue Française A Travers
L'Actualité Française
Industrial Archaeology — Survey of Hampshire, Dorset and the
   Isle of Wight
Workshop Course in Basic Electronics
Twentieth-Century Painting: The Expressionists and the Cubists
Discover Southampton
Education and Development in the Third World
The Mountain Environment
The Italian Renaissance
The Victorian Age
Diet and Drugs — Dilemmas and Dangers
Hampshire from Richard III to Elizabeth I
The Shaping of Post-War Southampton
Birds and Birdwatching
The 19th Century Novel in England, France and America
The Techniques of Field Archaeology
The Roman Empire
Literature between the Wars 1918—39
Alfred and Charlemagne
Ecology of Birds
The English Country House and Garden
Reading Greek for Pleasure
The Wheat and the Chaff: English Drama 1900—1930
From Resort to Port: Southampton in the Georgian and
   Victorian Eras

It is not just that women are channelled into certain 'feminine'
kinds of subject areas, but that within certain subject areas, women
do not appear to feature at all. The study of history, philosophy,
religion, art, music and literature is very much a consideration of
male interests and achievements. The social conditions which
produced such achievements and have accorded them so much
value and prestige are left unquestioned. Through this kind of
educational transmission in extramural and WEA classes both men
and women subscribe to the belief in female inferiority and male
supremacy. Nor is it simply a question of redressing a bias which

has largely ignored women's experience and exploits. Women have been, and continue to be, left out of the discourses which construct the knowledge that is considered valuable in the first place. Dorothy Smith puts it like this,

> Women have largely been excluded from the work of producing the forms of thought and the images and symbols in which thought is expressed and ordered. There is a circle effect. Men attend to and treat as significant what men say. The circle of men whose writing and talk was significant to each other extends backwards in time as far as our records reach. What men were doing was relevant to men, was written by men about men for men. Men listened and listen to what one another said. This is how a tradition is formed.[14]

The public rhetoric of adult education has consistently endorsed this view of the world, and whilst reforms have been envisaged, and occasionally even implemented, they have rarely addressed themselves to inequalities and discrimination based on gender. It has taken feminists within adult education; to provoke this debate — and, as we shall see, begin the massive task of redefining knowledge in the light of women's culture and experience. But first let us consider in more detail the tradition which has excluded us.

Within the early history of adult education, the middle years of the nineteenth century are seen as an important period in the development of working-class education. The struggle for social relevance and a curriculum related to social change were central concerns. Richard Johnson[15] has shown how popular politics from the corresponding societies of the 1790s to Chartism and the Owenite movement all had a lively educational purpose. So far as this tradition was concerned 'really useful knowledge' had to be 'real knowledge' which served practical ends. Johnson records some of its sentiments as outlined in the radical press of the early nineteenth century:

> This knowledge will be of the best kind because it will be practical.[16]
> All useful knowledge consists in the acquirement of ideas concerning our condition in life.[17]

What we want to be informed about is — how to get out of our present troubles.[18]

If manure be suffered to lie in idle heaps, it breeds stink and vermin. If properly diffused it vivifies and fertilizes. The same is true of capital and of knowledge. A monopoly of either breeds filth and abomination. A proper diffusion of them fills a country with joy and abundance.[19]

According to Johnson,

When radicals spoke of 'really useful knowledge' they meant most often one, or other, of all of these understandings . . . these understandings were powerful . . . they embraced, after all, a theory of exploitation in the economic realm, a theory of state power and oppression, a theory of cultural domination . . .[20]

But it was male knowledge that was the issue in all of these debates and when working men campaigned for the vote after 1860; it was manhood suffrage they were concerned about. For women, excluded from early trade union participation — except in their own organisations — and forced back into the home wherever possible, the assumptions about femininity that prevailed in society were based on a domestic ideology which located women well and truly in the home. What may have begun as a bourgeois convention had become general in patriarchal family relations, and by the second half of the nineteenth century was being pressed by the trade union movement in its campaign for a family wage and the protection of male jobs from female infiltration. The rationale was both aggressive and protective, as this speech by Henry Broadhurst to the TUC in 1877, makes clear:

They [the men] had the future of their country and children to consider, and it was their duty as men and husbands to use their utmost efforts to bring about a condition of things, where their wives would be in their proper sphere at home, instead of being dragged into competition for livelihood against the great and strong men of the world

Women were defined in relation to men, and as mothers and wives rather than workers or political activists. These assumptions had important implications when it came to definitions of 'really useful knowledge' and appropriate educational provision.

An early initiative, inspired by philanthropic and non-conformist concern to socialise the masses into acceptable levels of literacy and proper Christian duty, was the Sunday Schools movement. So far as the participation of working-class women was concerned, the benefits were seen as two-fold: their moral welfare would be protected and their household skills and child-rearing practices would be greatly improved. The notion of cultural and moral deficiency and the need for behaviour modification and domestic training was established almost from the beginning.

Mechanics' Institutes are usually regarded as one of the main developments in adult education provision during the nineteenth century. In their original conception they were not intended for working-class women, and those who gained access to them in the early days did so with considerable difficulty. When women were admitted they did not enjoy equal membership rights, and had to make do with restricted facilities. They generally paid lower subscription rates, and were excluded from the processes of decision-making which decided curriculum matters and Institute policy.

The number of women attending the Institutes varied. In northern industrial areas they rarely comprised more than a quarter of the members, but in some smaller Institutes and in the south women might represent as many as half or more of the total students.[21] It is by no means clear that these were working-class women, however. Since it now appears that mechanics' institutes largely failed in their intention of attracting working-class men, it seems unlikely that they were any more accessible to working-class women. In Manchester, for example, it was decided to attract women of the lower middle class — the daughters of shopkeepers and women from respectable but impoverished families who could not afford the fees for more expensive schools, and in Liverpool too, middle-class women predominated.[22]

The justification for extending adult education provision to women was based principally upon patriarchal assumptions about women's incompetence in those duties for which it was assumed they were inevitably responsible. Roland Detrosier, an earlier champion of education for working-class women, preached 'positive discrimination' in terms of improving their performance as wives and mothers.

Be assured, the conditions of the industrious artisan can never be permanently improved until the daughters of the poor can be educated to perform with propriety and decorum the important duties of a wife and mother . . . If it be essential to teach young men the principles of the arts and sciences, is it not equally essential to the comfort of man that young women should be taught the duties of housewifery?[23]

After 1840 it was common for special women's classes to be established in the Institutes — their curriculum to include the 'three Rs' and practical skills. Both were considered necessary because of women's prime responsibility for children and domestic management, as this comment in 1859 by Barnet Blake of the Yorkshire Union of Mechanics' Institutes makes clear:

As the first lessons of instruction, whether for good or evil are derived from the mother, it is evident that our young females should not be neglected. Upon their training depends much of the future, and indeed it has been asserted that if attention were specifically applied to the education of the female portion of our population, all the rest would follow as a matter of course. To reading and writing with the simple rules of arithmetic, should be added the indispensable art of plain needlework so necessary to the comfort of the working man's household[24]

When Working Men's Colleges were introduced in the second half of the century the same difficulties of access and inequality of conditions applied as in the Mechanics' Institutes, and it was still assumed that women would require different forms of education to suit their different temperaments and responsibilities.

In politics they would not be the same, nor perhaps in ethics. It is quite clear that women should have lessons in social life and order as well as in ethics, taking domestic life for the ground. They should also have lectures upon health, though I suppose the physician would feel the necessity of giving them an entirely different character from those he addressed to men.[25]

Given the origins of Working Men's Colleges in the Chartist and Christian socialist movements — with their emphasis on self-fulfilment through humane education and upon fellowship and brotherhood — perhaps we should not be surprised that, within a liberal-patriarchal ideology, the notion of fellowship was strictly masculine conception.

The curriculum for women was more restricted in its range than that offered to men, and the sense of separate needs was even more pronounced when women were educated on their own. In Halifax a women-only institute was established and in 1859 it was reported that,

> In the young-women's institute great progress has been made. A school of cookery has been instituted in which young women are taught the art of plain cooking, such as will increase the comforts of the home of the working man, and economise his limited means. They are also taught the art of cooking for the sick, which not only teaches them a lesson of charity, but also provides them with the means of usefulness in their own homes when sickness visits them.[26]

The discussion about 'really useful knowlege', which was so important to the male working-class tradition was, so far as women were concerned, *domestically* useful knowledge, and in this sense it did not really matter whether the providers were middle class or working class.

> If women entered an educational form where men were in the majority and where men mainly held the power to make policy decisions, then they tended to be denied equality of membership and equality of access to curriculum provision . . . if women were educated separately, there was always the risk that they would become confined to a cultural ghetto.[27]

Evening schools also made their first appearance in the middle of the nineteenth century. Frequently run by 'ladies', the classes offered instruction in the 'three Rs', sewing and religion. 'It was also hoped that cooking might be taught and that eventually vocal music and "other softening and sweetening arts" could be added'.[28]

Sewing schools sprang up in a number of towns, and in Leeds in 1860 it was reported that between 100 and 200 young factory women turned up each evening to learn skills which would enhance their prospects and performance as wives and mothers.[29] So far as working-class women were concerned, whatever their own aspirations might be, the curriculum that was offered was basic and limited by their domestic responsibilities and their role in the reproduction of labour.

In 1867 the first lectures in the university extension tradition began. They were intended for adults from both middle and working-class backgrounds, but were eagerly monopolised by middle-class women. There were no official barriers preventing access, and as today — so long as fees were paid and the class size was reasonable — all comers were welcome. The 'performance' of lecturers was highly consistent with middle-class university life, however, and Victorian conceptions of culture. In these circumstances it is not surprising that working-class men and women stayed away; as did middle-class men who, if they required such enlightenment, could enjoy it 'properly' as full time students.

The origins of the Women's Co-operative Guilds were initially rooted in the same kind of patriarchal values which defined women as domestic managers and consumers, and this was reflected in their early meetings and activities. But the organising secretary between 1889 and 1921 was Margaret Llewelyn Davies, a graduate of Girton College and the influence of Emily Davies, and she had a much broader view of education. By the beginning of the twentieth century guildswomen had become actively involved in the Co-operative movement in their own right and in local politics. For many, the guild was an opportunity for education, but also an initiation into socialism and women's rights. Guild members read widely and attended educational and women's rights conferences. The guild taught them

> what an immense power united action can be, and how the humblest may attain to its best form . . . It gave them confidence to stand up for themselves, to fight for maternity benefits, divorce, education, insurance and of course the vote; it 'brought them out' as they said themselves.[30]

Numbers swelled from 1500 members to 52,000. The curriculum was organised by working-class women at local level, and whilst domestic management may have been a part of the broad provision, great emphasis was placed on politics, economics and trade union rights. What began as yet another instrument of domestication was transformed, by the women themselves, into the conscience of the Co-operative movement; its members heavily committed to emancipation, minimum wage-rates, housing and divorce reform and the introduction of maternity benefits.

The struggle for education among working-class women — then

as now — was not achieved without male resistance, however. Classes that, within their content, could be guaranteed to 'enhance the home comforts of the working man', were of course not at issue, but educational activities which offered a new outlook on life and which in the process called into question masculine control over that life, provided the challenge that patriarchy could well do without. Mrs Layton comments,

> Sometimes my husband rather resented the teaching of the Guild. The fact that I was determined to assert my right to have the house in my name was against the Guild. The Guild, he said, was making women think too much for themselves. I did not quite agree with him there, though I did, and still do think, the Guild has been a means of making its members think more of themselves than ever they did before . . . It is impossible to say how much I owe to the Guild. It gave me education and recreation . . . From a shy nervous woman, the Guild made me a fighter.[31]

It is clear that for the first time, perhaps, a separatist, working-class organisation, committed to serious education and political issues affecting women, provided the opportunity which no other philanthropic or patriarchal provision had intended or succeeded in doing. It gave working-class women a voice, and the opportunity to use it free from male intimidation and middle-class patronage. Perhaps the secret of its success lay in its relevance to the material and cultural concerns of its members. They were not the targets for misplaced cultural imperialism orchestrated by the middle class in an attempt to civilise the masses, nor did they indulge in abstract intellectualism in mimicry of the universities. A characteristic feature of guild education — be it collecting information on various topics, preparing and reading reports at conferences or reading and discussing books of political interest — was that it was all bound up with appropriate action. The knowledge that was valued was useful in a real sense and it was also practical. The same can be said of trade union education. The history of women in trade unions has always been the history of a battle to establish the rights of women as 'workers'. Throughout the nineteenth century the majority of skilled unions excluded women in an attempt to protect the jobs, status and wage levels of male workers. Employers were keen to take advantage of developments in mechanisation which might enable them to replace skilled workers with cheaper (female) machine operatives, and to use women as strike-breakers. The solution was not to banish women from the unions, however, but to organise all workers effectively against the divisive strategies of employers. But working-class men no longer accepted that women had 'a right to work' — although many did in dirty, hazardous and sweated trades, usually considered 'women's work'. Women's place was in the home — as the earlier comment by Henry Broadhurst makes clear. The ideal was the bourgeois vision of 'the angel in the house', and the notion that women should be protected from the 'dangers' and 'moral temptations' involved — presumably — in mixing with men.

Not unnaturally, women were suspicious of the self-interested chivalry and misplaced moralism of their male colleagues and, excluded from male organisations, decided to form their own. Between 1874 and 1886 The Women's Protective and Provident Society (later to become the Women's Trade Union League) helped establish between 30 and 40 women's branches. Gradually, men realised that it was preferable to work alongside women in terms of union organisation, but not without considerable lobbying from the Women's League. The number of women in trade unions double between 1910 and 1914. In mixed unions the tradition of meetings in pubs and male-dominated committees was already established, but in women-only societies, and the recently formed National Federation of Women Workers (1906), women became used to taking responsibility and voicing their opinions. It wasn't until the First World War that unions generally opened their doors to women, although the Amalgamated Engineering Union (AEU) — despite women's employment in munitions and the like — excluded them from membership until 1943.

It is clear, however, that organising among women workers would not have developed to the extent it did without the impetus of the Women's Trade Union League and the initial energies of separatist organisations — a detail of history which is usually overlooked in discussions about positive action for women. Neither should it be forgotten that the traditions which introduced these developments displayed a healthy educational purpose as women, despite stereotypes associated with their 'natural inclinations' and 'proper sphere of influence', perfected the skills necessary to become practised negotiators, union activists and political organisers.[32]

The detailed history of adult education for working-class women in the nineteenth century has still to be written,[33] but the indications are that women faced a number of problems associated with their subordination under patriarchy. Patriarchal assumptions about domestic labour circumscribed their opportunities. Patriarchal control restricted their access to institutions and reflected limited ideas about what they might study. Apart from the Co-operative Guilds and the women's trade unions, there is little evidence of education concerned with anything other than basic accommodation to the sexual division of labour in the home, and the transmission of skills commensurate with the requirements of capital for cheap, unskilled secondary labour.

Notes

1. Annmarie Wolpe, 'Introduction to Fresh Horizons', *Feminist Review*, no. 6, 1980.

2. Jane L. Thompson (ed.) *Adult Education for a Change*, Hutchinson, 1980.

3. Edward and Enid Hutchinson, *Learning Later*, RKP, 1978.

4. See, for example, 'Adequacy of Provision', *Adult Education*, vol. 42, no. 6, 1970; Tom Lovett, *Adult Education, Community Development and the Working Class*, Ward Lock, 1975; P. Fordham, L. Randle and G. Poulton, *Learning Networks in Adult Education*, RKP, 1979.

5. Raymond Williams in *The Long Revolution* (Penguin, 1961) distinguishes four sets of educational philosophies and ideologies which rationalise different emphases in the selection of the content of curricula, and relates these to the social positions of those who held them. The liberal position he associates with the nineteenth-century aristocracy and gentry.

6. E.g. K. H. Lawson, 'Community Education: A Critical Assessment', *Adult Education*, vol. 50, no. 1.

7. *Adult Education A Plan for Development* (Russell Report) HMSO, 1973.

8. Geoff Brown, 'Independence and Incorporation: The Labour College Movement and the WEA Before The Second World War'; Mel Doyle, 'Reform and Reaction — the WEA post-Russell', both in Thompson (ed.) *Adult Education for a Change*.

9. Russell, *Adult Education*.

10. See Basil Bernstein, 'On The Classification and Framing of Educational Knowledge', in M. F. D. Young (ed.) *Knowledge and Control*, Collier–Macmillan, 1971.

11. Russell, *Adult Education*, and *Structure and Performance in Adult Education*, Harold Wiltshire and Graham Mee, Longman, 1978.

12. Sallie Westwood, 'Women and Adult Education', Open University, forthcoming.

13. Wiltshire and Mee, *Structure and Performance*.

14. Dorothy Smith, 'A Peculiar Eclipsing: Women's Exclusion form Man's Culture', *Women's Studies International Quarterly*, vol. 1, no. 4, 1978.

15. Richard Johnson, 'Really Useful Knowledge, Radical Education and Working-class Culture', in Clarke, Critcher, and Johnson (eds) *Working Class Culture*, Hutchinson, 1979.

16. *The Co-operator* (an early Owenite journal).

17. *The Pioneer* (an early Owenite union journal).

18. *The Poor Man's Guardian.*

19. *The Poor Man's Guardian.*

20. Richard Johnson, 'Really Useful Knowledge'.

21. June Purvis, 'Working-class Women and Adult Education in Nineteenth-century Britain', *History of Education*, vol. 9, no. 3, 1980.

22. Ibid.

23. An address delivered at the New Mechanics' Institute, Pool St, Manchester on 30 December, 1829, quoted in Purvis, ibid.

24. Report of the Yorkshire Union of Mechanics' Institutes, read at the 22 Annual Meeting, held in Rotherham, 15 June 1859.

25. M. E. Sadler (ed.) *Continuation Schools in England and Elsewhere: Their Place in the Educational System of an Industrial and Commercial State*, 1908.

26. Report of the Yorkshire Union of Mechanics' Institutes, 1859.

27. Purvis, 'Working-class Women and Adult Education'.

28. Ibid.

29. J. Hole, *Light, More Light. On the Present State of Education Amongst the Working Class of Leeds, and How It Can Best Be Improved*, 1860.

30. Margaret Llewelyn Davies (ed.) *'Life As We Have Known It' by Co-operative Working Women*, Virago, 1977.

31. Ibid.

32. See Labour Research Department, *Women in Trade Unions*, Allen and Unwin, 1919; Sheila Lewenhak, *Women and Trade Unions*, Ernest Benn Ltd, 1977; Sarah Boston, *Women Workers and the Trade Unions*, Davis-Poynter, 1980.

33. See Westwood, 'Women and Adult Education'.

6 ADULT EDUCATION THEORY AND PRACTICE — A FEMINIST CRITIQUE*

A number of official reports and publications have set the tone and caught the attitudes of those who have served as opinion leaders in adult education during the last seventy years or so, and whilst a detailed examination of these from a feminist point of view still needs to be undertaken, it is possible to identify a few preliminary characteristics.

A Design for Democracy — commonly called the 1919 Report — appeared at the end of the First World War in a spirit of high optimism. (Its tone is oozing with missionary zeal and enthusiasm for adult education.) Most of the twenty-one members of the committee that produced it came from the university extension movement and the WEA, but there were also representatives of the Co-operative movement, The Adult Schools, the YMCA and the Central Labour College. Albert Mansbridge and R. H. Tawney were members, as was Ernest Bevin. The chairman was Arthur Smith, Master of Balliol, and the secretary Arthur Greenwood, then Assistant Secretary to the Ministry of Reconstruction.

According to the report, adult education was to have an important place in the new Britain of the post war period and be closely related to the concerns of democracy, citizenship and life-enrichment. When reading the report, however, we are left in no doubt that the vision was of an essentially male utopia. Not that women were deliberately excluded — the report shows concern that, 'women have far less opportunity than men for continuing their education, owing to the increasing round of household duties and care of children'. and favours 'increasing educational facilities adapted to the peculiar difficulties and special circumstances of women', and at one point actually suggests that child-care facilities should be attached to classes. But Smith's prefatory letter to Lloyd George presenting his committee's findings and recommendations reflects the tone of the whole report. No doubt there will be some who argue that his use of the symbol of 'man' also embraces

*This chapter is substantially based on work by Nell Keddie and Sallie Westwood which was to be part of a joint paper. I am indebted to them for allowing me to drawn upon their material to a greater extent than the references indicate.

'woman', but I would not be one of them.

The adult, even when he has forgotten most of what he learnt at school before he was fourteen, cannot be put back to the spelling book and the multiplication table. In the interval between fourteen and eighteen he has been receiving an education, formless indeed and fragmentary, but emphatic enough, and in its way effective, the education of practical life. His adult education must be taken up at this point and on this plane. It must work from his existing evocation and interests, must begin by answering his existing inquiries and perplexities, and go on to the satisfaction of his aspirations. It must show him the reasons that underlie his daily work, the way in which that work has come to be arranged as it is, and how it can be arranged better, the relation of his work to that of others, and its place in the economics of the nation and of the world . . . He begins the study of economics not with the abstract definition of value and exchange, but from the insistent facts of his own wages, his own cost of living, and the aims of his own trade union . . . There is something about the mind of a man who has had no schooling from sixteen to eighteen which absolutely requires that the mental process shall begin by crystallising, as it were, about some visible palpable object . . .

A tutorial class consists of men who have felt the need and desire for such mental discipline so strongly that they have themselves formed a class and asked to be supplied with a teacher approved by themselves . . . Men who begin inarticulate, hardly able to read without a strain, come, in one or two sessions, to express themselves on paper with notable clearness and force. Above all, they learn from discussion with the teacher and with each other to rise above their original prejudices and limitations, to see that there are two sides to every question, to have an open mind and have a sense of the paramount duty of truth: that is, they are educated . . . The committee has based its conclusions upon the following propositions. That the main purpose of education is to fit a man for life, and therefore in a civilised community to fit him for his place as a member of that community.

That the essence of democracy being not passive but active participation by all in citizenship . . . he must learn . . . what his nation is and what it stands for in its past history and literature

. . . what are his duties to it . . . and the economic, political and international conditions on which his nation's efficiency and well being depend . . . for the furtherance of international co-operation in science, medicine, law, commerce, arts, and for the increasing establishment of world peace . . . the necessary conclusion is that adult education must not be regarded as a luxury for a few exceptional persons here and there, nor as a thing that only concerns a short span of early manhood but that adult education is a permanent national necessity, an inseparable aspect of citizenship, and therefore should be both universal and lifelong.

Considering that early recruits to the university extension movement were frequently women, and the WEA, although conceived as an association to advance the higher education of the working man, had a 50 per cent female membership when it came into existence[1] — this vision of 'the place of man' in a 'manly world' is a very partial view of both adult education at the time and of its students.

Just over fifty years later in 1973 came *Adult Education: A Plan for Development*, usually called the Russell Report. Two women were among the fourteen committee members chaired by Sir Lionel Russell and six assessors, although there is no evidence in their contribution to the report that they were feminists.

During the preceding twenty years or so, adult education seemed to many of those engaged in it, to have lost some of its earlier momentum. There had been no major review of provisions since the 1919 Report, and although the 1944 Education Act had been quite specific about the duties of local education authorities with regard to primary, secondary and further education, it did not actually mention adult education by name. All this contributed to the sense of insecurity and insignificance which many people felt about adult education, and why the policy statements made by Russell were seized upon with such eagerness and gratitude.

Given the close association of adult education in its formative years with voluntary and independent initiatives and with working-class education, and since the roots of the university extension movement and the WEA were well grounded in 'the special needs' of women and manual workers,[2] it is surprising to find the Russell Committee making no reference whatsoever to one of the most significant, voluntary, independent, educational, grass roots initiatives of recent years — the women's movement.

The re-emergence of feminism in Britain in and around 1968 was accompanied by a proliferation of informal meetings, study groups, 'consciousness raising', conferences, newsletters, publications, interpersonal conversations which, although related to campaigns and the concern to change the subordinate position of women in society, all reflected a serious educational purpose and commitment. Feminists within adult education have seen to it that adult-education classes increasingly reflect the interests of this important popular movement, but five years after its appearance, in the wake of similar developments in Europe and North America, and amidst considerable publicity and public discussion, the Russell Committee — defending more than a century of popular and political education — was completely oblivious to its significance.

The Russell Report, like its predecessor, favoured a definition of adult education as a 'process which continues throughout life', and called for a 'comprehensive and flexible' service. The report is probably most remembered for its championing of the cause of 'Disadvantage', and for its encouragement to the WEA particularly to get involved in work with socially and culturally deprived groups, trade union education and political education. The assumptions underpinning this concern are highly dubious, of course, and should be viewed more in terms of social control than either personal or political liberation[3] and it has been general, though not universally the case that the translation of these assumptions into practice has been repressive and therapeutic rather than radical and empowering.[4]

Women are rarely mentioned in the report, but when they are it is as 'mothers' — even 'working mothers' — rather than women that they are defined. A single sentence of the report calls for attention to the needs of women in industry, but whilst this is seen as important 'for their own intellectual progress' more significance is attached to 'their influence on their children'. The report says,

> The working mother is particularly important, perhaps with a special educational need, and as many more women will be at work in the coming decades, the influence of working mothers on children at the starting point of the whole learning process will spread widely. There will be a need for adult education to ensure that this is a supportive influence.[5]

It is noticeable that 'working fathers' are not charged with the same responsibility for the pre-school education of their children, and that women as full-time workers and major breadwinners in single-parent households, are still subsumed within the primary concept 'mother'. As Sallie Westwood comments,

> It is a familiar call and one that has been located within a discourse which places women firmly in the domestic sphere, wherein their performance in mothering will be judged by psychologists, social workers and others who pronounce upon 'the problem' of working mothers and the effects on their children.[6]

She suggests that the same discourses may be found within the language of the Russell report.

The other — but undeveloped — context in which women are mentioned is as statistics. The Russell Report is very meticulous in its presentation of statistics. The report notes that women outnumber men in LEA classes by three to one;[7] that women outnumber men in all types of courses except residential and training courses, in which the proportion of men is considerably higher;[8] and that the increase in women students over the years is greater than for men.[9] A subject breakdown gives detailed information about how many students are engaged in different courses, and reveals that only in social studies and science do men outnumber women.[10] Of course, we should not be surprised that men monopolise those areas of knowledge which, when the report was written, were most prestigious or, like science, specifically associated with male competence. Or that whilst the commitment of women might help to keep alive the 'bread and butter provision' of non-vocational evening and daytime classes, only those without domestic responsibilities and with vocational aspirations — i.e. men — could easily take advantage of the more costly, more time-consuming and more prestigious residential and training courses.

But Russell does not make these connections, or consider the extent to which adult education is merely replicating the unequal distribution of knowledge and educational opportunities characteristic of the wider education system. The predominance of women in non-vocational adult and further education classes represents the only circumstance within the whole of the education system in which women are in the majority. This is not, of course, unrelated to the fact that non-vocational adult and further education is the least valued and most miserably resourced outpost of education. However, women *do* constitute the majority, and instead of this being considered a weakness and a symptom of the marginality of adult education, it could be seen as a strength. If nothing else, it provides the context for women to meet, to validate their own experience, generate their own knowledge, become their own teachers and take control of their own learning — much as the Co-operative guildswomen did. The problem is that all this smacks of feminism, and whatever the rhetoric of adult education might be about 'flexibility' and 'responding to students' needs', the numerical significance of women in adult education and the cultural and political implications of this, are either ignored or simply not understood by the men who sit on official committees.

It is one of the contradictions of adult education that whilst a significant majority of the students are female — and a good proportion of the part-time tutors as well, especially in LEA provision — the organisation and provision of classes takes very little account of the social, economic, cultural and political conditions of being female in our society. The career structure, the responsibility for organisation and control, the arbiters of the curriculum, and the opinion leaders and policy-makers who sit on bodies like the Russell Committee are invariably men — men who operate firmly and squarely within the organisational structures, the cultural assumptions and the thinly disguised prejudices of patriarchal society. It is for reasons like these that so far as Russell was concerned, women were visible only as mothers, and totally invisible in every other respect.

In 1978 Graham Mee and Harold Wiltshire produced their report *Structure and Performance in Adult Education*.[11] Their investigation makes clear that, despite claims to the contrary about 'meeting individual need' and 'responsiveness to local communities and conditions', an amazing consensus exists throughout LEA non-vocational adult education about what kinds of programmes ought to be offered. Wiltshire and Mee do not utilise the classification 'women's interests' which appears in countless Institute prospectuses and Centre programmes, preferring 'crafts and arts', 'physical activities', 'cognitive studies' and the like. In practice 'women's interests' overlap a number of their categories and might — had this been appreciated — have made for more interesting and disturbing reading.

As an illustration, LEA provision in Southampton during 1981–2 offered day and evening classes in the following practical subjects — the vast majority of them concerned with domestic management or personal appearance.

Cake Decoration	Jewellery and Enamelling
Car Maintenance	Lacemaking
Canework	Machine Knitting
Clock and Watch Repair	Macrame
Cookery	Make Do and Mend
Creative Embroidery	Make Up and Beauty Care
Crochet	Metal Work
Crochet and Tatting	Mixed Crafts
Dressmaking	Navigation
Design and Pattern Cutting	Needlecraft
Fabric and Thread Workshop	Needle Rug Making
Fine Metal Crafts	Patchwork
Floral Art	Patchwork (Fabric Workshop)
Flower Arrangement	Photography
Fly Tying	Skin Care and Make Up
Gardening	Soft Furnishing
Gardening (Indoor)	Spinning
Glass Engraving	Tailoring
Handyperson's Course	Upholstery
Hostess Cookery and Flower	Wine and Beer Making
Arrangement	Woodwork
Jewellery	

LEA provision is frequently criticised for being merely 'recreational' and not 'educational'. A publication of 1963 by the Northern Advisory Council for Further Education offering 'Suggestions for Part Time Teachers of Women's Subjects' declares that women attend evening classes because of,

> the desire for the company of others and a change from household duties . . . this recreational attitude and motive is perhaps even more potent in the country than in towns for it is in rural districts that the evening class provides women with one of their few chances of meeting their friends and neighbours.[12]

'Keeping women off the streets' is an insufficient reason to protect adult education from cuts in public expenditure, however, especially if these are also middle-class women who attend adult education classes 'for leisure frills' rather than 'genuine' social need. Russell was sensitive to allegations of this kind.

> At times, especially when economies were being sought, there has been a tendency, even in official pronouncements, to depreciate many of these subjects as 'recreational' and therefore of little educational value, to assume that people go for social intercourse rather than to learn, and to dismiss certain kinds of activities as pandering to petit bourgeois aspirations.[13]

In an unpublished paper,[14] Nell Keddie draws attention to the way in which the more recent cuts in public spending 'have revived anxiety about how to defend adult education against the attacks of hostile education officers and councillors that adult education is no more than "leisure frills" for middle class women'. In noting that 'The symbolic focus for these attacks and for the anxiety they provoke are classes in cake icing and flower arranging', she argues:

> The central issue which is not confronted is that these subjects represent an adult education curriculum which is heavily biased towards a 'women's interest' curriculum (this includes a range of subjects not so obviously related to women's work) and it is presumably a reluctance to acknowledge this that renders adult education unable to provide a cogent rationale for these subjects. . . . To challenge the charge on its own grounds and to question whether these subjects can properly be described as 'leisure' activities would call into question the appropriateness of the claim that it is a 'recreative' curriculum when so large a proportion of classes are aimed at enhancing women's occupational skills in managing a home and servicing a family.
>
> The public rhetoric of adult education claims that it is a *universalistic* service which provides for the whole community and we can see that the attacks on cake icing and flower arranging threaten to expose the limitations of this claim. To confront it adequately would expose not only that women are the main users of adult education but that the LEA curriculum is strongly located in the home and in women's activities and not in leisure activities — which are of necessity male-orientated since women's work rarely permits the clear boundaries between work and non-work that the use of the term leisure usually implies.[15]

Keddie argues that the claim that adult education is a universalistic service serves to render invisible its preoccupation with women in their familial roles. She suggests, however, that the stereotype of the typical student 'appears to recognise the predominance of women in the student body since it draws upon the negative stereotype of women as passive, dependent, lacking in confidence and, in arenas of public life, lacking in social skills'. The claim from adult education that it is concerned with creating confidence in its students needs to be looked at very carefully:

> Confidence for what or in what? Is adult education, through providing a 'women's interest' curriculum, enabling women to become more satisfied consumers of their own oppression? Is it making them more confident and competent managers of their homes, more able to cope with its tensions through courses in Yoga, slimmer and more attractive through Keep Fit and Beauty Culture, and meeting their needs for self-expression through classes in painting or creative writing? Does providing women with an interest outside the home and a crèche for classes, give them a break from the children which makes them happier mothers and create more lively and informed wives who can show more interest in their husband's work?[16]

The philosophy of 'starting where the student is' may also too often leave her there — in the home, without substantially increasing the range of options open to her. Keddie comments:

> Adult education in its educational ideology, to an extraordinary degree, claims to be concerned with the relational and developmental aspects of learning . . . Women are experienced in servicing the needs of others rather than looking to their own self-development. It is ironic that both as students and as teachers on in-service courses, the self developmental programmes they are offered are in fact geared towards making them more competent in servicing others' needs. In this sense adult education seeks to penetrate family life and play a role in maintaining the sexual division of labour.[17]

When the attention of providers is directed at working-class women 'in the community', in 'outreach work' or in 'adult basic education' schemes, a further element becomes seemingly obligatory: child development and parent craft. For those who are 'isolated', 'unable to cope', 'bad managers' and pejoratively described as 'single parents', relevance and the development of skills is regularly defined in terms of being 'better mothers'. So that despite claims about 'individuality', 'personal development' and 'educational self-fulfillment' so beloved by adult educators, where women are concerned, it is as appendages of homes, husbands and children that they are usually assessed and catered for.

And the pattern is remarkably common throughout the whole of LEA provision. Wiltshire and Mee[18] hesitate to explain, and indeed claim 'not to know what the processes are that determine and maintain this consensus, or what the channels are through which they operate'.

The common denominator, of course, is the power of men in the context of a male management and career structure and range of ideologies about sex to decide what shall be taught and why. LEA adult education contributes in no small way to the confirmation of the sexual division of labour in the family — to the detriment of women's personal development and to the exclusion of other roles. The suggestion that women might see the world differently or might deny the values and standards determined by men, appears incomprehensible to those well used to 'meeting individual needs' and supplying 'confidence' in remarkably predictable and sexist ways.

In October 1977 the Secretary of State for Education asked the Advisory Council for Adult and Continuing Education 'to advise on the best way of building on the Adult Literacy Campaign in order to create and implement a coherent strategy for the basic education of adults'. A committee of the council met under the chairmanship of Henry Arthur Jones, and in March 1979 presented *A Strategy For the Basic Education of Adults*. The report estimated a population of at least three million people in Britain who are 'severely disadvantaged by lack of basic education skills', and recommended that an Adult Basic Education Unit be set up operated by a development board to co-ordinate and stimulate the provision of basic education and training — consisting of literacy, oracy, numeracy, English as a second language and coping or life skills.

As is general, the report describes and discusses a particular component of adult and continuing education — basic education — without any reference to the fact that the majority of students, volunteers and paid teachers engaged in adult and basic education are female. As usual, women remain invisible in the eyes of those who pronounce upon the theory and practice of adult education.

However, the language in which adult education is discussed and justified does imply that the female nature of the student population is, at a subconscious level, well registered in the spokes*men's* minds. Adult education, it is claimed, 'builds confidence', 'meets needs', 'assists personal growth and development' and 'starts where the student is'. These are never the justifications used to legitimise vocational training or subject specialisms in higher education, and it is worth considering whether, if the student population were predominently male, the same language would be used.

The 'feminine' nature of the objectives are not to women's advantage, however, because they rely on a male construction of female need, in circumstances in which men are the providers and need-meeters, and women are the recipients. As with the sexual division of labour generally, the adult education relationship is essentially a relationship of female tutor and students' subordination to male organisation and control. In the process, women's *real* needs (i.e. the definition *women* would make about themselves and their lives if men were not around or if men were not structually in charge) are not being recognised or met. It is not distractions that women seek, but space; not confidence, but autonomy.

To return to the report on basic education, if the lack of *specific* discussion about women masks subconscious assumptions about women — which are then *generalised* to apply to 'adults' or 'students' — it is worth considering the implications of what is being argued and advocated by re-focusing *specifically* on women. Let us assume that the report *is*, as it pretends *not to be*, actually, in reality, principally concerned with women. And if, as we have seen, it is women who are likely to have been least well served by their initial experience of schooling, and women who are most likely to be the majority of students volunteers and teachers engaged in adult basic education, then, if it is not labouring the point too much, quite reasonable to assume that it is women, either consciously or subconsciously, that Jones and his committee are actually concerned with.

Put into this perspective the report is really very worrying, because the picture which emerges is of feckless, pathetic, unconfident individuals, in need of remedial education and behaviour modification, encoded in the kind of coping-and-caring courses

offered to less able and less amenable pupils in schools. The classic
stereotype is that of under-socialisation, and although basic
education may offer some rewards to individuals, 'for the group as
a whole, it offers very little that can ameliorate the circumstances
of individual lives or the conditions which produce them'.[19]

The report has already been criticised for its failure to take any
account of social class and the distribution of economic resources
in society which produces structural poverty, inequality, unemployment and disadvantage.[20] Those of, 'the hidden and largely
defeated population whom life has taught to keep their heads down
and not expect much'[21] are presented as individuals suffering from
a series of afflictions which are regrettable and unfortunate, but
essentially the result of their own ineptitude. As Nell Keddie makes
clear the 'needs' of the disadvantaged are

> prescriptively defined by the educators in terms of the educators'
> perception of those needs, a perception which derives from *a
> concept of disadvantage which seeks to remedy social problems
> through the imputed inadequacies of individuals* . . . what this
> kind of explanation achieves in practice is a severing of the con-
> nections between the *political* nature of social problems and the
> individual who presents problems which, if they are severe
> enough, or sufficiently troublesome to others, will be dealt with
> as individual problems by the social workers, the police, the
> remedial teacher, or others of those whom Everett Hughes has
> called the 'dirty workers' of our society, meaning they do its
> dirty work for it.[22]

It is hard to escape the force of Keddie's argument in the face of
'unemployment' in the report presented as a problem of 'lack of
skill'[23] with basic education offered as a remedy, 'to counter the
loss of personal dignity, the waste of human resources and the
vulnerability to political extremism that hopeless unemployment
can bring'.[24] The aim is clearly to contain possible resistance and
act as

> a system . . . whose task is to repair the damage done to human
> beings by the way of life the social system entails for them: its
> function thus being inevitably corrective rather than
> preventative.[25]

But if the report takes no account of the implications of structural class divisions, neither does it recognise the social constructions of female inequality achieved by the sexual division of labour within the family, and the implications this has for the subordination of women. In this respect 'coping and life skills' concerned to assist in 'domestic management'[26] and 'health and family relationships'[27] will do little except confirm women in an exaggerated commitment to the propriety of their traditional roles. If women really are disadvantaged because of limited opportunities or poverty, or their social-class position or their subordination to men, learning to cope — to put up with — unsatisfactory circumstances defined as an essential life skill is most definitely not the kind of repressive remediation we should be promoting.

Notes

1. M. Stocks, *The Workers' Educational Association: 'The First 50 Years'*, Allen and Unwin, 1953.

2. Ibid; and *Adult Education: A Plan for Development* (The Russell Report), HMSO, 1973.

3. Jane L. Thompson, 'Adult Education and the Disadvantaged', in Jane L. Thompson (ed.) *Adult Education for a Change*, Hutchinson, 1980.

4. Mel Doyle, 'Reform and Reaction — the WEA Post Russell', in Thompson (ed.) *Adult Education for a Change*.

5. Russell Report.

6. Sallie Westwood, 'Women and Adult Education', Open University, forthcoming.

7. Russell Report, pt. 1, para. 83.

8. Ibid, pt. 2, para. 36.

9. Ibid, pt. 2, para. 36.

10. Ibid, pt. 2, para. 38.

11. Harold Wiltshire and Graham Mee, *Structure and Performance in Adult Education*, Longman, 1978.

12. Northern Advisory Council for Further Education, *Suggestions for Part Time Teachers of Women's Subjects*, Fourth Edition, 1963.

13. Russell Report.

14. Nell Keddie, 'Adult Education — A Women's Service?', unpublished paper.

15. Ibid.

16. Ibid.

17. Ibid.

18. Wiltshire and Mee, *Structure and Performance*.

19. Nell Keddie, 'Adult Education: An Ideology of Individualism', in Thompson (ed.) *Adult Education for a Change*.

20. Jane L. Thompson, 'Adult Education and the Disadvantaged', and Nell Keddie 'Adult Education: An Ideology of Individualism', in Thompson (ed.) *Adult Education for a Change*.

21. ACACE, *A Strategy for the Basic Education of Adults*, 1979.

22. Keddie, 'Adult Education: An Ideology of Individualism'.

23. ACACE, *A Strategy for Basic Education*, para. 8.

24. Ibid.

25. Ingleby, *The Psychology of Child Psychology*, quoted in Keddie, 'Adult Education'.

26. ACACE, *A Strategy for Basic Education*, para. 20a.

27. Ibid., para. 20d.

7 CONTINUING EDUCATION REVIEWED

The increasing popularity in recent years of the notion of continuing education has broadened the scope of discussions about education for adults beyond the limited definition we in Britain usually associate with adult education. The provision of adult education by the universities, the WEA and LEAs represents probably the least fashionable and certainly the cheapest range of educational opportunities available to adults. I do not mean to suggest, however, that such provision is unimportant — indeed the substance of this book is a commentary on the possibilities which it affords — but that discussion about *continuing* education enables us to consider the whole range of post-school education and training available to adults in a much wider context.

It is a concept used to encompass both education and training, vocational and general education, formal and less formal systems of provision — a provision which the Advisory Council for Adult and Continuing Education sees,

> not as another education 'sector' to march beside the administratively distinct areas of school, further and higher education, but as a conjunction of policies, funding, provision, and attitudes, to promote changes in all the present education sectors to the advantage of a rapidly growing number of adult learners.[1]

Elsewhere the same concept is referred to as 'lifelong learning', 'recurrent education' and 'education permanente'.

In this spirit a subcommittee of the Council produced in 1982 a report entitled, *Continuing Education: From Policies to Practice.* The report is premised on the two assumptions that all adults should be entitled to continuing opportunities for education throughout their lives, and that the education of adults should be given increased priority in the allocation of resources.

The report sets out proposals for developments which will take us into the twenty-first century, and in its scope includes reference to adult learning in universities, polytechnics, institutes of higher education, further education colleges, adult and community centres, schools, at home, at work and wherever else learning can take place. Immediately then, we are faced with a much further-reaching discussion than that restricted to notions of non-vocational provision or adult basic education. The report exhorts all educational institutions to recognise their responsibility for continuing education and to agree some common purpose. It suggests practical ways in which the full range of educational opportunities can be extended to adults throughout their lives, and underlines the belief that, both now and in the future, the education of adults should be taken at least as seriously as the education of children.

There are a number of factors encouraging this interest in continuing education. One is the imputed consequences of techno-logical change which, it is argued, will require a flexible and mobile labour force, and a total reconstruction of our basic assumptions about work and leisure. The promise of continuing education is seen as, 'a route to adaptability in a world where it is no longer possible to rely on the knowledge and skills acquired in youth'.[2] A second factor is the problem deriving from an apparent 'education gap', in which the opportunities available to the young continually outstrip the opportunities which were available to a previous generation.

> the present inequalities of our society which can adversely affect the relationships between government and people, and between management and employees, partly reflect the inequalities in the past and present provision of educational opportunities: the widening of these opportunities would help reduce these inequalities.[3]

It is considered inadequate to think of education as an initial and finite process in preparation for adult life: rather, adult education should continually reappear in people's lives in tune with their changing needs and inclinations. 'Nobody should leave school feeling that their education is finished'.[4]

The third factor is more pragmatic. The effects of a decline in the birth-rate have encouraged some educational institutions to look more favourably upon mature students as a means of off-setting the expected losses in eighteen-year-old recruits. Current govern-ment policies are demonstrating quite clearly that the ancient immunity from financial restraint and job insecurity enjoyed by those working in higher education can no longer be guaranteed. In these circumstances the defensive pressures on institutions to maintain student numbers is high, but the opportunities afforded to government by falling rolls to reduce expenditure and make cuts in provision is also — in the present climate — too attractive an opportunity to miss. Within this contradiction lies the major discontinuity between policy and practice with respect to continuing education. Student numbers are being cut — especially in arts and social science departments which traditionally attract high numbers of women applicants; subject areas which are unfashionable in the present climate, like sociology and educational studies, are in retreat; and discretionary grants, those paid to students without formal entry qualifications (mostly mature students), are an increasing casualty of cuts in local authority spending. The inflexibility of separatist institutions which recognise few methods of credit transfer between each other, and the restrictions on the mobility of mature women students with domestic responsibilities, are all factors limiting opportunities in higher education, despite the rhetoric of 'lifelong learning'. As Naomi McIntosh has said,

> Even though there is an increased demand for equality of educational opportunity from minorities and an increased demand from majorities (given that both women and the working class are majorities of any population) . . . at the same time the economic climate, the recession, unemployment, fewer jobs, make this difficult. While changing technologies require more education, while there is the likelihood of increased leisure, of people living longer, all these trends pointing towards greater provision of education for adults; at the same time the financial side is restricted. Does paying for education depend on increasing the wealth of the country or (more cynically) will it be cheap at the price to allow people to have more education when we haven't enough jobs to occupy them?[5]

The general assumption throughout the report, of course, is that education is 'a good thing' and the more one gets of it the better-off one will be. This is certainly an assumption which we should not take for granted. We are back to the question of access again and the nature of patriarchal education. Even if women do considerably increase their access to the opportunities previously monopolised by men in systems of education created and controlled by men, this will do very little to alter the basic relations between women and men in society. It is not merely a question of improving the chances of women to compete in a man's world — to supplement existing provision to that end — but to demand a radical change in the nature of what is being offered. This implies at least an equal share in its control, at least an equal share in the determination of what counts as valuable knowledge within it, and at least an equal recognition that what is important about women's experience of the world is as valid as men's. Without such *real* equalities, notions of 'equality of opportunity' are essentially rhetorical.

The major interest so far in discussions about continuing education has been the emphasis on work-related training. In Britain new developments, perhaps not surprisingly, have taken place outside the official education system through the auspices of the Manpower Services Commission (MSC). According to Annmarie Wolpe

> The MSC programmes have been extensive, innovatory and imaginative. From a modest beginning the MSC has mushroomed into an enormous organisation conducting research, coordinating the work of all the industrial training boards, initiating new schemes, buying courses in FE colleges, developing training programmes for older workers and schemes for unemployed youth.[6]

MSC courses have also been subject to considerable criticism too, of course, not least by those who view education as a direct replication of capitalist labour relations, and who regard any 'innovation' controlled by the Department of Employment, in the service of a capitalist–conservative state, as highly dubious. We have seen MSC money used in quite pragmatic ways in recent years to distract attention away from the increasing seriousness of unemployment and to provide a number of short term palliatives. And though the work of the Training Services Department in developing Training Opportunities courses has been praised, so far as women are concerned the opportunities have been restricted almost exclusively to preparation for traditionally female employment in clerical, secretarial and office work.

Eric Robinson, opening the joint Equal Opportunities Commission (EOC) — University of Manchester conference on 'New

Opportunities and Second Chance Education for Women' in 1978 — claimed that, 'This nation spends much more on the education and training of men than women'.[7] He went on to describe how the policies of national and local government were intensifying the problem, and charged further and higher education institutions with being 'masculine in conception' and 'inflexible in their attitudes'.

The EOC has amassed considerable evidence to the effect that training opportunities for women are insubstantial in quantity and predictable in quality. There is little evidence to suggest that the successful completion of such courses increases women's employment prospects or earning power, especially in circumstances in which women who return to work have few options but to accept the jobs which are available — mostly unskilled and badly paid. Women's work in the service sector has contracted in recent years, social work and teacher-training opportunities have been cut and nursing 'as a vocation' continues to register perhaps the highest level of professional exploitation. Unemployment among women continues at almost twice the male rate, but is either ignored, disguised or dissipated within moralistic exhortations about restoring motherhood to its place of honour and returning mothers to 'their proper place' at home.

With women's traditional work precarious, and mothering presented as a moral imperative, the much applauded re-training schemes have offered few alternatives to women seeking new skills with which to anticipate new careers in non-traditional employment. The Equal Pay Act of 1975 has proved meaningless in circumstances in which women do not generally have the opportunity to secure the jobs which merit equal pay with men; and a Sex Discrimination Act (1975) and an EOC which cannot legally require employers, trade unions and educational establishments to implement positive action programmes, or exercise positive discrimination in favour of women, are largely irrelevant in the struggle for real, as distinct from rhetorical, change.

The introduction of new technology so far as women are concerned has also been disastrous. The advance publicity was of course highly seductive, 'We were told it would improve the quality of our lives, give us more leisure, make our jobs more streamlined, cleaner and more pleasant, make Britain prosper again'.[8] In reality the automation of the office, for example, and the introduction of word processors and visual display units (VDU), has, and will have, spectacular effects on women's jobs and women's health.

Emma Bird, investigating the impact of new technologies, reported to the EOC that 64,000 word processors would be installed in British offices by 1985, of which one in three would replace a worker.[9] APEX, the office workers' union, puts the total of job losses even higher. Evidence gathered so far from America, Britain and Sweden suggests that the predictions are absolutely right.[10] Also worrying are the implications for the health of the workers who will be retained to operate the new machines. Rachael Grossman has described the working conditions of women producing and testing micro-electronic chips in South-East Asian factories,

> After three or four years of peering through a microscope, a workers' vision begins to blur so she can no longer meet the production quota. Workers who must dip components in acids and rub them with solvents frequently experience burns, dizziness, nausea, sometimes even losing their fingers in accidents. It will be ten or fifteen years before the carcinogenic effects begin to show up on the women who work with them now.[11]

Hazel Downing has described the health hazards endemic in the working life of VDU operators in Britain and the United States,

> By closing off the natural breaks that typists have with a traditional typewriter — such as changing the paper, even shifting the margin — the work around word processing increases stress and fatigue. The experience of stress is not just related to bad posture and uninterrupted performance of a single task (keyboarding), it is also the result of pressure to increase or keep up with standard productivity rates. Associated problems can also occur, but their link to the VDU can only, in the absence of adequate medical research, remain speculative. Carroll, for instance, told me that during the five years she worked at the bank, out of thirty pregnancies there were only two normal births. The abnormalities included a high rate of miscarriage, physical deformities on birth (club feet, improperly placed hip bone, in one case no hip bone at all, and cleft palates). After about three years using the machines, there was a lot of people experiencing colour distortion and more opacity in vision, they

couldn't quite see as clearly and things didn't appear as bright as they used to.[12]

Downing's research also presents a graphic and horrific picture of automated drudgery in which women, plugged in by a set of earphones and connected to a centralised dictating system, become, as keyboard operators, part of the production line.

> Secretarial people didn't like them because they already had the skills and the pay, but the novelty of course, you know everybody was excited to learn this new thing that was going to help alleviate boredom and make life easier, and . . .
> HD: Those were the promises?
> Right, right. And then they found out that they really didn't do that at all — in fact they made it more boring . . . Because people felt that they were plugged into machines, that they were appendages to machines rather than people performing functions with other people . . . We used to have jokes about how we expected that soon they'd chain us to our desks and give us catheters so we'd never have to go to the bathroom. (Laughter) And the thing is that once word processing or video display equipment is introduced it's possible to keep track expertly of the amount of productivity each individual displays and set raises and evaluations accordingly. And people feel very pressured to get out their production. The standards are raised. When I first started at the bank, the standards were 8,000 keystrokes an hour and when I left they were 12,000 over a five-year period of time. (Carroll, WP operator in a large American bank in San Francisco)[13]

The extent to which MSC is merely training women for skills which are fast becoming obsolete, and is not engaged in alternatives, means, as Annmarie Wolpe points out, 'The aims embedded in continuing education can only be applied to men (since) nowhere are provisions seriously being made for women as a group in the light of the developments of new technology.[14] In discussing the specific problems faced by women in securing opportunities for continuing education, Naomi McIntosh presents a picture of opportunities worsening rather than improving.[15] She is sceptical about separate provision for women, which she sees as a retreat from the more important task of altering society to enable women to take their opportunities equally, side by side with men; but her evidence is of women increasingly losing high-status jobs in education, business, industry and the media to men, and as the victims of both formal discrimination and of being 'outsiders' in the 'old boys' network'. Even the importance attached to securing paid educational leave (PEL) for British workers could, she points out, work to the disadvantage of women because developments of this kind will only assist those in full employment. The temporary, transitional and part-time nature of a good deal of women's work will serve to exclude them from PEL and could widen the discrepancies between men and women in this respect.

There is one small light amidst the general gloom, however, which, if we are to accept Gramsci's optimism, can be a focus for development. Gramsci[16] was convinced that despite the all-pervasive power of ruling groups, which he called hegemony, education has an important part to play in challenging its ubiquity — especially adult education, which he regarded as political education. Gramsci's analysis was formulated in the context of factory councils and working-class industrial struggles, but the same conviction that education has the potential to affect political consciousness holds good. For women the opportunity of education can be enormously significant. Annmarie Wolpe argues that education, 'can increase women's individual consciousness in terms of their own abilities and potentials: and perhaps more importantly, can increase their overall understanding of women's situation within the broad social spectrum',[17] and Tessa Blackstone, that, 'better-educated women are more likely to be politically active, to believe in sex equality, and to be less likely to avoid situations of conflict'.[18] For these reasons recent innovations in adult education opportunities for women have to be protected and expanded. Important in this respect are those courses which encourage women to anticipate new roles.

Helen Hootsman[19] summarises the main development in re-entry to work and study programmes for women in Europe in terms of five general categories:

(1) Courses stressing social—cultural orientation
(2) Courses leading to qualifications or diplomas at the secondary school or university level
(3) Courses for (re)entry to work or study, often called 'threshold' programmes.

(4) Vocational training, especially in non-traditional fields

(5) Management and Leadership training.

She provides a number of examples:

Social–cultural orientation . . .

The changing role of women in society is usually the theme of non-formal and non-credit discussion courses that seek to give women an overview of current issues in society and of their own relationship to these issues. A successful model is the 'Women Orienting in Society' programme (VOS) which started in 1974 in North Holland as an emancipatory experiment for women who had only one or two years of secondary school. The programme struck a responsive chord across the Netherlands. Now, about 600 courses are given in neighbourhood centres and peoples universities . . .

Courses for High School/University Qualifications . . .

In the United Kingdom, a striking example of second-chance learning that offers an excellent opportunity for women (even though not designed specifically for them) is the Open University, founded in 1971. Every resident, aged 21 or over, is eligible to study without presenting a qualifying diploma. The OU offers the alternatives of studying for a BA degree, taking a single course or doing research for a higher degree. Most courses involve ten months of part-time study. Students can attend study centres for tutorials and counselling during the course as well as attend summer schools in particular fields. In 1978 there were about 75,000 people (a large percentage of them women) studying with the Open University: a further 27,000 had already obtained their degrees . . .

Courses for (Re) Entry to Work . . .

In Germany a number of Volkshochschulen offer general orientation courses for (re) entry to work, such as the Professional Orientation for Women course at VHS Charlottenburg (Berlin) or Frauen Zurück in dem Beruf (Women Back to World) at the Tiergarten (Berlin) Folk High School. In Ireland, ANCO, the Industrial Training Authority's Return to Work course for Women established in 1977, is designed to help mature women (aged 25–55) who had not worked outside the home for some time to adjust to the world of paid employment. This ten-week full-time orientation course, currently being offered in five training centres, concentrates on social and career planning and job finding skills and includes a seven-week period of work experience. Normal Training Centre procedures apply in all areas with the exception that the classes start a half an hour earlier to accommodate those who have to make arrangements for the care of children. The women receive a training allowance of £35–£40 a week with additional allowances for dependents, travel and subsistence where applicable . . .

(Re) Entry to Study . . .

Among the many (re) entry provisions for further study is the Fresh Horizons programme in London. Founded two years after the first US model at George Washington University, called Developing New Horizons, the course offers mature students a broadly based general education programme without formal entry requirements. Subjects studied include literature, mathematics, social studies, spoken and written English, speech and drama. A counselling and advisory service is available. The central point of the course is to give women the confidence to reach the point where they can 'appreciate and consider new opportunities open to them'. While some women decide to return to work, the larger group opt for degree courses, some prepare for vocational training in the social services and teaching, others in higher education . . .

Vocational Training to Enter Non-traditional Fields . . .

The Gothenburg Folk High School in Sweden offers a twenty-week course for women to learn carpentry and repair work. Sweden has other innovations. The labour market training programme is an important factor in extending educational opportunities for women. The training aims at qualifying workers for new occupations and industries and also at strengthening their long-term labour-market positions by including required courses in Swedish and English, mathematics, physics, chemistry and civics. Such courses are of particular value to women who have not completed their formal education. (A similar labour-market training programme in Norway has an enrolment of 6,738 participants (3,386 women) in 82 types of courses during 1977–8).

Management and Professional Training . . .

Noticeably absent from the list of provisions for women are the fields of professional management training. Not yet as popular in Western Europe are the kind of US programmes offered by

Foothills 'New View' in California or the certificate courses of the Continuing Education Centre for women at George Washington University. Nor have European governments widely introduced experiments with affirmative action for the employment of women comparable to the United States' Civil Services Upward Mobility Programme or the Women's Programme of the Federal Government. The German Marshall Fund of the United States has taken the initiative to promote management training for European women by offering 15 scholarships (three for the academic year 1980–81) at the French School of Management. The fund hopes to be able to stimulate business support for the continuation of this project. A number of women's organisations are also concerned with the dearth of such managerial opportunities and have requested government assistance in various countries to set up short term projects.

Encouraged by legislation promoting affirmative action programmes for women, innovatory projects in the United States have also been impressive. Oonagh Hartnett[20] identifies five main developments:

(1) The creation of institutes or centres attached to universities which conduct research on such topics as the economic status of women, problems relating to blue-collar and trade union women, educational equity and, in general, the changing roles of men and women, and the implications for individual behaviour and the functioning of organisations and institutions . . .

(2) The establishment of Women's Studies courses. These may be multi-disciplinary or may concentrate upon such subjects as the Psychology or Sociology of Women, Women and History, Women and Science, Women and Literature, Women and Education. The courses are academic in content and may lead to a major at undergraduate level or, more rarely, to a master's degree. Courses are now beginning to be established at the secondary school level as well. They represent an intelligent search for and discovery of new insights that are challenging predominantly male-centred curricula . . .

(3) The setting-up of professionally oriented courses. These range from full-time courses that may last a calendar year,

through to full time courses for a few weeks or months, to part-time courses and week-end workshops. They cover clerical and blue-collar, professional and technical jobs: there is at least one which trains women for work inside trade unions . . .

(4) The emergence of special leadership training courses for women who wish to take an active role in public life . . .

(5) Courses bridging the transition from home to work or further education or between a less senior and more senior job . . . They are aimed at: increasing self-awareness, sense of personal identity, autonomy; reducing any guilt women may have in resuming work; helping women become (more pro-active about their life/career plan and feel more in charge of their lives. The courses are run by a variety of organisations including women's centres, community colleges, women's organisations, private non-profit organisations, profit-making consultancy agencies, and by the extension or outreach units of universities.

In Britain perhaps the most important development has been in the growth and proliferation of Women's Studies courses inspired by feminism and the women's movement, and currently making an enormous contribution to the task of learning liberation. I shall consider the implications of these courses in more detail in subsequent chapters. The other, and partly related, development has been in courses variously referred to as New Opportunities for Women (NOW) Wider Opportunities for Women (WOW), Fresh Start, Fresh Horizons and Second Chance. Trail-blazers have been initiated by the City Literary Institute in London, (Fresh Horizons) Hatfield Polytechnic (NOW), the WEA and the Universities of Newcastle and Durham (NOW), and Liverpool University and the WEA (Second Chance). There are probably as many as thirty or forty similar courses currently being offered in different parts of Britain.

NOW courses are, as the name suggests, confined to women, and in Newcastle at least, have emerged very clearly from the tradition of university adult education. The entry is open and non-selective, students study in tutorial groups subjects like literature, history, philosophy and sociology; they are sometimes taught by men and in a manner reminiscent of the 'great tradition' with no immediate concern for qualifications. However the courses are considerably longer — 60 sessions in 20 weeks — compared to the more usual 10 or 20-session classes, and in addition to academic study, they offer help with study skills, personal and career counselling and information about further education and employment opportunities.

Ruth Michaels describes the NOW course at Hatfield Polytechnic as one offering,

> a comprehensive guide to the mature woman who may wish to return to active working life but is unsure or unaware of how best to do so. It aims to help the student to become acquainted with the opportunities that exist for re-entry to education, or retraining, for part time or full time employment, second careers or voluntary service. The course also helps the student to gain new self-confidence, become more aware of new horizons and establish long term goals based on her individual interests, abilities and aspirations.[21]

The academic and informational aspects of the course are closely related to preparation for further education or employment, and there is strong emphasis throughout the course on counselling and guidance support. The experiences of running NOW courses over a ten-year period has, according to Michaels, had a profound influence on the provision of continuing education in the polytechnic. Preparatory courses for entry to degree-level work have been arranged, and experiments based on the Swedish tradition which allows adults to enrol for single courses of a degree programme, have enabled some women to become associate students of the polytechnic, studying units for their own enjoyment or in preparation for a degree. A BA in Cultural Studies offered by the polytechnic was specifically inspired by the needs of NOW students. Students can 'step off' along the way with a certificate, a diploma or a degree. They can leave at any point and return later to continue to a higher award. The emphasis is on flexibility, and every effort is made to recognise that the life and work-patterns of mature women require that they should not be treated for administrative convenience, like 18-year-old male school leavers.

The Fresh Horizons courses emanating from the City Literary Institute in London are open to men and women, but women considerably outnumber the men. Again, they are very much within the liberal tradition of general education, and have not, in the same way as Women's Studies has done, challenged the selection and transmission of male-centred knowledge which is consistent with that tradition. Fresh Horizons students like NOW students can generally expect to engage the kind of learning about the kind of information which the male academic tradition has long reserved principally as its own. In this sense neither course is specifically feminist, and yet the opportunity of education in circumstances which take women's right to education seriously, and which acknowledge women's domestic responsibilities, but which do not define women in terms of them, can have a politicising and consciousness-raising effect. Alice Lovell,[22] herself a Fresh Horizons student, describes the course as one intended for people wanting to make a fresh start in education. The occasion that encourages many women to enrol, however, is an attempt to shift the direction of their lives — perhaps after a divorce or when children leave home. The experience of being with other mature students engaged in a common endeavour encourages a process of self-examination which can be a kind of consciousness raising in itself. For many the course can act as 'a catalyst in the process of resocialisation', and provides the stimulus and sense of self-respect necessary to contemplate and achieve new roles.

If increased political awareness and a greater sense of personal autonomy are some of the 'unintended' consequences of Fresh Horizons — part of the course's hidden curriculum — the declaration of political intent is much more an explicit and concentrated feature of the Second Chance to Learn programme organised by Liverpool University Institute of Extension Studies and the WEA. The course is open to men and women and has been running since 1976. Its roots are very much in working-class education in Liverpool, in community action and the trade union movement, and whilst a central concern of the course is to provide entry into further and higher education for those who want it, equally important is the opportunity to consolidate working-class cultural experience and to develop skills which assist in political action relevant to the material condition of working-class life.[23] Race discrimination, unemployment, labour relations, and sexual politics provide the context in which student's life experiences become the curriculum of the course — the tutor's role is one of clarification and consolidation rather than cultural imposition. The language is not of 'liberal education', 'guidance' and 'counselling', but of solidarity with the material and political interests of working-class people. Although sponsored by the university and the WEA,

Second Chance to Learn is part of a different adult education tradition from the one which has inspired Fresh Horizons and the Newcastle courses. It is in the tradition of independent working-class education: of Robert Owen, the Chartists, The Plebs League and the National Council of Labour Colleges. So far as women are concerned it is essentially a male tradition as we have seen, and the close links with local trade unions and shop stewards' committees has the possible effect of continuing to incorporate women's experience within the general concerns of working-class struggles. However, half of the students each year are women, and the politics of the course keeps close links with community-action groups and women conscious of the additional oppression that gender and race contribute to working-class conditions. These connections seem to have prevented the worst aspects of patriarchal domination taking hold. And as Liz Cousins comments, 'It is interesting to note that women students on Second Chance are much more likely to remain to the end of the course'.[24]

Courses like these provide the opportunity for women to reassess their lives and to contemplate new roles and changing circumstances. All of them report considerable student commitment and enthusiasm, and seem to be helpful and constructive in a way which is relevant to women re-entering education and paid employment. As such they should be supported and extended. Courses like these do not operate in a social and political vacuum, however, and it is important to realise their limitations in the context of a society still controlled by men and an economic system which would be profoundly challenged by women claiming the right to work on the same terms as men. The ideology of domesticity and the structural arrangements concerned to impede the progress towards equality for women, remain dominant. In this respect the re-entry courses we have just considered have two major weaknesses.

In general — and except in Liverpool — they remain relatively inaccessible to working-class women. One of the students interviewed by Alice Lovell, who in fact left the Fresh Horizons course feeling depressed and disenchanted, said,

Older working-class women have been given little opportunity to learn about mathematics, physics and other subjects. Lack of confidence is a built-in condition through the poor and narrow education grudgingly supplied them and through social attitudes. The majority of other students on the course are middle class educationally and socially — more than enough to scare working-class women away.[25]

This is not to deny that middle-class women may have equally valid and important reasons for needing to shift their lives in a new direction — indeed they do — but educational provision has always been monopolised by middle-class groups, and used as a way of consolidating their relative power and comfort in society. The education system reflects middle-class values and reinforces middle-class cultural norms. An important struggle for working-class groups is to gain equal access to the educational institutions they help to pay for and have a right to attend, but not at the expense of working-class culture, working-class interests and working-class political concerns. Every effort should be made to engage working-class women in the opportunities that are available, but with the assurance that what is offered reflects a proper critique of capitalist and patriarchal control, and assists in the development of skills concerned to resist their consequences.

The second related weakness is the limitation built into the notion of role education — of any description. We have seen that women will remain disadvantaged so long as decisions about their education are taken in the light of restricted social stereotypes about their 'natural inclinations' and 'proper sphere of influence' — stereotypes which confirm women in close allegiance to their domestic and traditional roles and which have been principally arranged to suit the interests of capitalist patriarchy. However, if a new role in education or a new role as a working wife merely constructs other restrictions and other behavioural expectations, we may only have replaced one stereotype with another, one master for another.

The experience of women returning to study or returning to employment is rarely so clear cut. They find themselves pulled between competing responsibilities and competing expectations — the bridge, which Donna Kate Rushin describes,[26] between everyone, but woman and her own true self.[27] The short-term solution turns out to be the attempt to combine roles, to work a double shift at home and outside the home, two jobs for the price of one, both of them full time and yet each inextricably part time. Alice Lovell found that, 'married women were "allowed" to continue academic work but not at the expense of their household duties . . .' and whilst women may wish to expand their horizons beyond the domestic field and beyond the part-time labour force, men do not usually exhibit a similar desire to scrub their own floors and wash their own shirts (let alone anyone else's). Until they can be made to accept a radical change in their life style, the most that women will achieve will be the right to be part-timers in both areas.[28]

The long-term solution is more difficult, and is concerned with the need to escape from the restrictions implied by the notion of role — especially when the prescriptions are mediated through the self-interested concern of men. As women, we scarcely know what we can potentially be — so used are we to being defined and circumscribed by our relationships with men. To accept a new role in their world is to accept merely a different restriction.

Unless women think much more deeply about themselves, make sense of their experience and expectations in reference to their own needs and interests, and consider strategies for redefining the relationships with men in ways which will change the distribution of power and oppression to one of equality and respect, learning new roles will continue to be a poor substitute for the practice of freedom and liberation.

Notes

1. ACACE, *Continuing Education — From Policies to Practice*, 1982.
2. Ibid.
3. Ibid.
4. Ibid.
5. Naomi McIntosh, 'Education for Women in United Kingdom, in *Women and Adult Education: Learning New Roles for a Changing World*, European Bureau of Adult Education, 1981.
6. Annmarie Wolpe, 'Introduction to Fresh Horizons', *Feminist Review*, no. 6, 1980.
7. EOC, *New Opportunities and Second Chance Education for Women*, 1979.
8. Anna Coote and Beatrix Campbell, *Sweet Freedom*, Picador, 1982.
9. Emma Bird, *Information Technology in the Office: The Impact on Women's Jobs*, EOC, 1980.
10. Hazel Downing, 'Developments in Secretarial Labour: Resistance, Office Automation and the Transformation of Patriarchal Relations of Control', (unpublished PhD thesis), Centre for Contemporary Cultural Studies, University of Birmingham, 1981.
11. Rachael Grossman, 'Changing Role of S.E. Asian Women', *S.E. Asia Chronicle, Pacific Research*, SRC, no. 66/PSC vol. 9(5).
12. Downing, 'Developments in Secretarial Labour'.
13. Ibid.

14. Wolpe, 'Introduction to Fresh Horizons'.

15. McIntosh, 'Education for Women'.

16. Q. Hoare and G. Navell Smith (eds) *Selections from the Prison Notebooks of Antonio Gramsci*, Lawrence and Wishart, 1971.

17. Wolpe, 'Introduction to Fresh Horizons'.

18. Tessa Blackstone, 'The Education of Girls Today', in Juliet Mitchell and Ann Oakley (eds) *The Rights and Wrongs of Women*, Penguin, 1976.

19. Helen Hootsman, 'Educational and Employment Opportunities for Women — Main Issues in Adult Education in Europe', *Convergence*, ICAE, vol. XIII, no. 1–2, 1980.

20. Oonagh Hartnett, 'Transition from Home to Work: Some Training Efforts in the USA', ibid.

21. Ruth Michaels in EOC, *New Opportunities*.

22. Alice Lovell, 'Fresh Horizons: The Aspirations and Problems of Intending Mature Students', *Feminist Review*, no. 6, 1980.

23. Martin Yarnit, 'Second Chance to Learn, Liverpool; Class and Adult Education', in Jane L. Thompson (ed.) *Adult Education for a Change*, Hutchinson, 1980.

24. Liz Cousins, *I'm a New Woman Now: Education for Women in Liverpool*, EOC, 1982.

25. Lovell, 'Fresh Horizons'.

26. See also Chapter 10.

27. See Chapter 10 below.

28. Lovell, 'Fresh Horizons'.

8 WOMEN'S STUDIES AS AN ALTERNATIVE MODEL IN ADULT EDUCATION

The growth and development of Women's Studies courses have been a fairly recent phenomenon and it is difficult to be sure just how much activity is going on. There have been few statistical studies which have outlined the growth of Women's Studies generally, and no comprehensive surveys or reports to establish the breadth and depth of teaching and research related to women. In 1974 the Feminist Press in America produced *'Who's Who and Where in Women's Studies'*, and listed 4,658 Women's Studies courses taught by 2,964 teachers. In Britain The Women's Research and Resources Centre produced a guide to Women's Studies courses in the UK in 1981. It is by no means comprehensive, and is concerned more to indicate the kinds of courses that are happening, rather than quantify the extent of the development.

The Centre also keeps a record of research projects being undertaken by feminists and concerning women — many of which are being carried out independently and outside the usual academic channels and institutions. The sense is certainly of a much bigger development and greater amount of activity than official statements, conferences and publications indicate, but then with the official arm of adult and continuing education firmly controlled by men, and dominated by male professional interests, we should not be too surprised at this state of affairs.

The emergence of Women's Studies has been a direct consequence of the re-emergence of feminism and the growth and development of the women's movement during the last two decades, the women's movement has provided the context in which meetings, study groups, 'consciousness raising', conferences, newsletters and publications have been the seedbed for educational activities which have only subsequently become the concern of more formal educational initiatives. The development of Women's Studies reflects one of the main concerns of the women's movement not to have the material, political and spiritual culture of women any longer deleted from the records kept by men.

The fact that women of other periods have been as concerned about the position of women as ourselves, and have lived lives as women very different to the lived experiences of men, have not been immediately apparent to us. It has taken persistent, dedicated effort to clear aside the obtrusive overgrowth of male questions, feelings, concerns, theories, explanations and recommendations that passes for the totality of recorded wisdom and human culture, to reveal women. It has meant examining the assumptions which have enabled legal, medical and scientific knowledge to trivialise and distort both the concerns and conditions of women's lives, and to represent dubious prejudices about women's sexuality, intellect and temperament, for example, as authentic reputable scholarship. The criticism made by Otto Rank in 1958 about psychology that it is 'not only man made . . . but masculine in its mentality'[1] has been increasingly applied to all other disciplines including the so-called natural sciences.[2] And the starting point has been women's own experience. When it did not conform to the version presented by men the version was questioned, including the assumption of the right to create inaccurate knowledge about women in the first place, and the interests which might be served by so doing.

So long as men have been powerful, they have used their power to describe the world in their own terms; to create, confirm and reinforce the knowledge which has concerned them historically. Clearly this does not imply an easily comfortable consensus. The construction of male-centred knowledge has, of course, been the product of political and social conflict as well as resistance and suppression. The construction of male-centred knowledge has also taken place in the context of unequal economic resources and vastly different social conditions between races and classes of men. In most respects it has been the knowledge of white, upper and middle-class men which has triumphed at the expense of poor and black men. But at another level, the struggle has been between people of a similar kind — between *men*. They may have disagreed and argued and even fought wars with each other to be able to run things their own way, but their battle ultimately has not been about change but about keeping things the same. Individual and collective acts of rebellion have often demonstrated courage and frequently satisfied the need for change, but the values and rights which were being defended — the values and rights of *men* to shape and determine the world — have remained the same.

Women have not usually been part of these deliberations. The history of humankind has been a history of the progressive elimination of women from the public counsels and public affairs of men.

What might in the very beginning have been a function of biological difference with respect to child bearing, has been reinforced by a massive programme of social construction and engineering throughout recorded history to arrive at a condition which has nothing whatsoever to do with biology. It is not biology but the suppression of ourselves as women which is at the heart of our powerlessness. Each development — economic, political, ideological — has increased the ubiquity of male power, and institutionalised it into systems of inequality which are presented by those who have created and who control them as 'normal', 'natural' and 'inevitable'.

A major consequence of this — beside the most obvious relegation of women to a subsidiary position — is the related defamation and discrimination which has accompanied the social construction of women's inequality. Denied access to male deliberations and the distribution of power, we women have become the victims of decisions made *for* us and of definitions *about* us. Men have historically defined our inferiority, originally in terms of biology, and more recently according to the seemingly 'more objective' measurements of science, medicine, law and culture. They have also been 'the experts' on our character, our emotions, our needs and our feelings. *They* have told *us* what we think. And when what they have said does not comply with what *we feel* — and we have been brave enough to object — we have been variously dismissed as 'unstable', 'hysterical', 'mischievous' or 'abnormal'. Our foremothers — and there have been many who resented the subjection of women to the rule of men — have been repeatedly discredited as either deficient or deviant in some way and punished accordingly.[3] Also, their many testimonies and their triumphs in the face of considerable odds have been short-lived, never recorded, or deleted from the records by continuous male indifference.

Women's Studies is a commitment to not letting that process of deletion continue, but also to a study of the process itself, and of the assumptions and arguments which have made it possible for men to assume that they have the right to disempower and discredit us, to discount our own knowledge and to create wrong information about us in the first place.

It is not merely a question of writing women back into the history books and reclaiming our culture. We women do need a reorganisation of knowledge of perspectives and analytical tools that can help us know our foremothers, evaluate our present historical, political and personal situation, and take ourselves seriously as the agents of the creation of a more balanced culture.[4] But merely adapting the record to highlight the achievements of celebrated women — however refreshing it may be to discover that some women have done more than they are given credit for — will do nothing to redress the implicit sexism of the law, for example, or to alter the ideology which has kept medicine, government and science as essentially masculine preserves. Nor will it have very much to say about 'uncelebrated' women's lives or the processes which have operated historically and materially to control and suppress women.

Whilst no one is suggesting that the entire apparatus of men's knowledge and the male academic tradition be discounted and dismantled, the implication of Women's Studies is that we need a radical redefinition of subject matter, different lines of enquiry and new ways of learning. The prospect is not an 'academic exercise' with a new 'body of knowledge' to construct into a subject, and to make respectable with certification, research and publications in much the same way as other selections have been fashioned into specialisms, (although there are dangers here which I shall return to presently), but about *a process of learning* concerned to empower women and to change fundamental attitudes and behaviour. Minnie Bruce Pratt writing about rebellion, and discussing the urgent need for disobedient behaviour to challenge the power of patriarchy, says,

> I understood years later that my mother and grandmothers and great grandmothers had been heroines, in one way, and had used their will to grit their teeth and endure, to walk through the ruins, blood and mess left by men. I understood finally that *this heroic will to endure is still not the same as the will to change, the true rebellion.*[5] (Bruce Pratt's italics)

In this spirit we need to maintain a constantly militant and critical stance against the power of patriarchy and its concern to silence us, a challenge which needs to be taken into the places which employ us as well as into the hearts and minds of our fellow students as together we learn and practise liberation.

Women's Studies courses come in many forms. In the United States by far the biggest development has been within colleges and universities, with rather less evidence of developments involving community women in non-formal learning situations. Since colleges and universities are, by definition, elitist institutions, this has led to some concern about the inaccessibility of Women's Studies to poor, black and Third World women.

In 1980 University of Kent offered the first British Master's course in Women's Studies, although it has been possible to take Women's Studies options in a number of other postgraduate and undergraduate degrees.[6] By definition these programmes do not accept the present position of women in society, and are concerned to heighten female awareness about the processes of subordination as a necessary corollary to social action. By offering alternative explanations of social and economic organisation historically and currently, the courses challenge the legitimacy of existing power structures. Housed within the academy they also question the academic traditions and presentation of knowledge which discount women and which perpetuate the celebration and practice of patriarchal attitudes and power. The challenge to the so-called objectivity of male knowledge calls into question not merely the content and construction of particular subjects, but also the relationship between subjects and the values of 'specialism', 'excellence' and 'authority' which are ascribed to them.

It is no coincidence that Women's Studies in Britain have been organised in extramural departments and through the channels of the WEA more readily and more easily than within the university. Once Women's Studies are acredited with academic status and resources within universities, they offer not merely a discreet view on the world within the confines of a 'new subject specialism', but a commentary on the rest of the curriculum and of academia. This has led to some resistance.[7] The non-vocational, non-examined, and non-statutory nature of adult education classes seems immediately more conducive to the philosophy and practice of Women's Studies, although developments have not been established without resistance in these areas, either.[8]

Courses vary enormously. The WEA has been responsible for stimulating a good number of discussion groups reminiscent of the 'consciousness-raising' activities of the women's movement and concerned to provide a focus for discussion about the immediate experiences of women's oppression. Often these have been centred on neighbourhood women's groups, in community meeting places and other informal settings. Sometimes they have been arranged in conjunction with Women's Liberation and Women's Aid groups and have marked the close association with political movements which the WEA historically and, at its best, still considers to be important. Courses organised by university extramural departments have a tendency to be more 'profound' in their intention and to be a catalyst between critical awareness and substantial analysis. These are typical of those organised by the University of London, Department of Extra Mural Studies in 1981/2.

'Too Pretty to be Serious' — Images of Women, Alison Weir, Lamorbey Park, AEC, Sidcup.
Who is this myth of a human being? Was she created by man? We trace woman from the times when she was legally inferior — how did she handle this supposed total subjection? We study the 'Gag' woman, gagged and gagging, as we look at playwrights, novelists, poets, saints, politicians, at how women had to be to succeed. From Julian of Norwich to *The Lacemaker*, from Polly Peachum to Polly Garter, from Aphra Benn to Pam Gems, from silent stitchers of the Bayeux tapestry to Mary Quant, we look at woman in her true form.
Language and Gender: An Exploration of our Individuality, Geraldine Lander, Goldsmith's College.
'Dear God' wrote Anna, 'are boys better than girls? I know you are one but try to be fair'. The course will look at the different ways in which language itself constructs and signals dominant man/subordinate woman images which influence our consciousness. What can we do about it?
Women and Housing, Helen Austerberry and Sophie Watson, City Literary Institute.
This course is designed to examine how the lives of women are affected by housing policy and housing design. The assumption that the nuclear family is the basic social unit is increasingly questioned as the number of single women and women alone with children increases. Among topics to be covered in both historical and contemporary aspects will be women's economic position in relation to housing tenure and access; housework and housing design; women and homelessness; women's aid and housing; council housing and the effects of sales and allocation on women.
Psychoanalysis and Female Identity, Ann Scott, Camden AEI, Haverstock School.
Psychoanalysis has always aroused controversy, whether within

feminist, marxist or therapeutic circles. How best can we assess what it tells us about motivation, our mental life and the construction of individual identity? We will work this out by looking historically and thematically at the major psychoanalytic writings on female identity, sexuality and 'femininity'. Topics covered will include Freud's essays and case studies on hysteria and feminity; the early psychoanalytic debates and the current feminist interest in Freud, Lacan and Klein.

The Angel in the House? Images of Women in History, Marcia Millman, 32 Tavistock Square, WC1.

Women have traditionally been seen in history as inhabiting the domestic sphere. The Church, the law and the state have defined them as dependents, primarily as wives and mothers. How have these definitions changed over time? How has this affected how women see themselves? How did they resist these definitions and seek change? Such questions will be explored through discussion of the family, maternity, work and sexuality and the ways in which women challenged these through trade unions, birth control, educational and suffrage organisations.

Freer from the constraints of qualifications and academic regulations, adult education has proved a much more sympathetic and appropriate base for the introduction and experimentation implied by Women's Studies. Adult education, with its origins in independent working-class education; its historic concern for non-statutory provision and characterised, to some extent in the WEA, by student control, is proving to be an important connecting point between the informal expression of feminist demands and dissatisfactions, and the translation of these into political and cultural practices which consolidate the growing rejection of patriarchal authority by increasing numbers of women.

Of course, the conventional wisdom of opinion leaders in adult education reflects a complacency about the relative enlightenment of provision compared to further and higher education and compulsory schooling. Because of its special character, accessibility to women, sensitivity to students and voluntary commitment, it is frequently assumed that adult education cannot be subjected to the same kind of feminist criticisms that are made about other forms of education. As we have seen, this is far from the truth. But adult education does have the potential to be different. Its rhetoric about flexibility, personal growth and non-hierarchical structures is eminently suited to the characteristics of the women's movement and its associated educational activities. Feminists have been able to exploit this rhetoric to win resources and spaces within adult education for Women's Studies, although the developments have not been without struggle, as we shall see, largely because of the discrepancy between rhetoric and reality. Also adult education is the least prestigious and most under-resourced outpost of the education system. In a good year less than 1 per cent of the education budget is devoted to it. In times of recession and during recent years, cuts in public spending on education have bitten deeply into an already impecunious provision; in some areas it has been cut back dramatically, in others the fees have been increased to the point of prohibition. In talking about the penetration of adult education by Women's Studies, therefore, we have to remember that in real terms we are talking about a highly marginal development — though not an insignificant one. Although there is a good deal of variety in Women's Studies courses, the approaches used rely heavily on the important characteristics of feminism and the women's movement which conceived them. Some may focus specifically on history or literature or law or economics for example — and it is certainly important to re-examine and reconstruct the subject matter of traditional disciplines from the perspective of women's lives and women's concerns — but increasingly it has become clear that the fragmentation of knowledge into discreet specialisms is itself part of the process of patriarchal practice which needs to be challenged. Mary Daly talks of

The tyranny of methodolatry, which hinders new discoveries. It prevents us from raising questions never asked before and from being illuminated by ideas that do not fit into pre-established boxes and forms. . . . Under patriarchy Method has wiped out women's questions so totally that even women have not been able to hear and formulate our own questions to meet our own experiences.[9]

Women's Studies has increasingly challenged traditional disciplines and subject boundaries, and the fragmentation of knowledge which

weakens thought and permits the secure ignorance of the specialist to protect him from the applications of his theories. It is difficult to imagine a woman-centred curriculum where quantitative method and technical reason would continue to be allowed to become the means for the reduction of human lives, and where specialisation would continue to be used to escape from wholeness.[10]

Women's Studies are by definition, then, inter-disciplinary, reflecting the women's movement's fight for wholeness. They also reflect other important concerns. To begin with, the learning is controlled by women, not men, and that which is regarded as useful, crucial and important knowledge comes first from women's own experience of the world. Unlike traditional education, which has stressed the neutrality and objectivity of knowledge and sought to de-personalise scholarship, learning in the women's movement has claimed value and validity for the experience of all women. A second characteristic is the spirit of equality which the women's movement encourages in favour of the hierarchical and oppressive power relationships characteristic of capitalist and patriarchal systems. In terms of learning, this makes hierarchical distinctions between women inappropriate, as are notions of merit, elitism and competitive self-interest. By taking a more open and flexible stance the women's movement has been able to take seriously the feelings of all women and to accommodate the similarity, variety, diversity and contradictions of our different experiences of the world. In this respect notions of expert knowledge and the mystique of leadership have been profoundly challenged by women taking more and more responsibility, developing skills and exerting increased control over their own lives in ways rarely permitted under patriarchy. The conviction that any woman can do a whole range of things which traditional socialisation and education preclude has been an important ingredient in the development of self-esteem, autonomy and collective strength. This means that learning also becomes a communal enterprise in which the distinctions between teachers and students become increasingly meaningless. All women have something to teach and something to learn. In this respect the characteristics of female talk and communication styles — undervalued and misdirected within patriarchy — take on new significance.

Phyllis Chesler has commented[11] on the extent to which women listen and men talk and Zimmerman and West[12] on the extent to which men dominate and interrupt in mixed-sex conversations.

Pamela Fishman[13] argues that women do 'the shitwork' in conversation — they feed men the lines, draw them out, respond to the topics that men determine and act as their audience.

> There is a division of labour in conversation, though the women generally do more work, the men usually control the conversations that couples have. Since the men's remarks develop into conversations more often than the women's, men end up defining what will be talked about and which aspects of reality are the most important.

They also talk more — roughly two-thirds of the time, according to Dale Spender.[14]

Women have generally been so silenced by their experience of male-dominated education that even 'the successes' of that system, the women who transfer to college and university, usually make their presence felt essentially in silence. As Adrienne Rich says,

> Look at a classroom, look at the many kinds of women's faces, postures, expressions. Listen to the women's voices. Listen to the silences, the unasked questions, the blanks. Listen to the small soft voices, often courageously trying to speak up, voices of women taught early that tones of confidence, challenge, anger, of assertiveness, are strident and unfeminine. Listen to the voices of the women and the voices of the men; observe the space men allow themselves, physically and verbally, the male assumption that people will listen, even when the majority of the group is female. Look at the faces of the silent, and of those who speak. Listen to a woman groping for language in which to express what is on her mind, sensing that the terms of academic discourse are not her language, trying to cut down her thought to the dimension of a discourse not intended for her (for it is not fitting that a woman speak in public); or reading her paper aloud at breakneck speed, throwing her words away, deprecating her own work by a reflex pre-judgement: I do not deserve to take up time and space.[15]

The implications of all this are not that women should talk more or copy the adversary and abrasive style favoured by men, but that women's talk should be revalued. As should the activity of listening. 'If listening were shown to be as important and as complex as talking, and if it were shown to be equally valuable, there would be repercussions in all our social institutions'.[16]

The facilitating, listening, turn-taking talk of women has not been invented as a method in Women's Studies discussions, although it is characteristic of these discussions. The discussions reflect the same careful attention to others characteristic of 'consciousness-raising' groups in the women's movement which are in themselves a reflection of the ways women left to themselves, usually talk to each other. Talk between women, long discounted by men as trivia or gossip, has been historically the site of female friendship and support.[17] Talk between women, without the presence of men, and without the pressure to respond to men's language and to provide the emotional management of male egos, can be subversive and revolutionary. Revolutionary in that it is based on different values and can redefine relationships; and subversive in that it provides the opportunity to speak the thoughts women frequently keep to themselves when men are around. Although women habitually defer to men in conversation, this does not mean that they also accept and believe everything they say. When we speak of our disbelief and confirm our lack of acceptance to other women, there begins the practice of disobedience which has the power to destroy collusion. Judith Mullard puts it like this,

> It seems to me that learning with women — and I can't delineate here between being in a women's group or in a women's studies course or being with women I love — is the ultimate challenge to male knowledge and, therefore, eventually to their control — to learn in an open feminist way where you don't have to hide what you're saying where you don't have to cope with two kinds of reality, theirs and ours, where every woman's experience is valid and where what you did today, or decide to do tomorrow, can be an assault on patriarchy — it feels like it must have done unlacing your stays.[18]

Dale Spender argues[19] that the opportunity for women to talk together to validate their own experience and to generate a new knowledge in a relationship of equality, which discounts the notion of leadership, and which has a catholic view of expertise, provides a powerful learning experience which is central to Women's Studies, but which is less acceptable within traditional education.

This is understandable in one sense because if the learning experiences of the women's movement were to find their way into traditional education, no males, no class and no ethnic group would be dis-proportionately successful, and education would look very different.[20]

Learning together with women can also be challenging to men in another way. It can accentuate the friendship and solidarity between women that the women's movement calls sisterhood.

I think being with women and learning together is very threatening to men. I don't just mean men feel threatened by it — they do and they ought to, because once women start on that process, start questioning, coming up with answers, re-defining and generating our own knowledge, it must irrevocably alter the relationships between men and women politically and personally. But what is even more threatening is actually choosing women's company, not just 'going on a course' or 'going to a group' but wanting to be with women socially and doing things together, that really challenges notions of family togetherness. In lots of family situations I know it isn't possible but even in ones in which it can't be openly criticised it's really difficult because to say one wants to do it all the time (and I do) seems like a rejection of the family (and in a sense it is).[21]

This of course leads to the other key principle — the close association between theory and practice, a link which is not always well made, or indeed encouraged, in traditional education. Keith Jackson has continually argued the need to take the social, political and economic conditions of working-class students seriously, and that relevance in the curriculum should be explicitly defined as class relevance. He has also argued that,

The problem with most liberal adult education since the Second World War is that it has concentrated on satisfying intellectual needs alone. With a few notable exceptions, including some adult education for trade unionists and industrial workers, it has been too far removed from the processes by which ordinary men and women can meet their collective economic and social needs.[22]

One of the characteristics of the women's movement is, to borrow the publicity from a well-known popular novel,[23] its capacity to 'change lives'. The learning experience within the women's movement has never been a purely intellectual or educational affair, but directly related to personal and collective growth, development and change, and to a whole range of campaigns and political activities concerned to challenge and alter women's subordinate position in society. That same link between action, continually developed and interpreted through interaction with theory, and described so eloquently by Paulo Friere[24] as a kind of personal praxis, also serves as a model for feminist studies. It is inconceivable to imagine courses which value women's personal experience, which develop an alternative version of women's lives to the one which legitimises their oppression, and which encourage women to stop denying their own interests in the service of patriarchy, as courses bound by the usual liberal reluctance to be 'where the action is' when students decide to take their learning out of the classroom and into the home, the picket line or the political arena.

For women concerned about change it is important to remember Emma Goldman's observation that the way we make our revolution determines how and who we shall be after it. The responsibilities are enormous not only to our own true selves but to each other. As teachers we have two choices:

> to lend our weight to the forces that indoctrinate women to passivity, self-deprecation, and a sense of powerlessness . . . or to consider what we have to work against, as well as with, in ourselves, in our students, in the content of the curriculum, in the structure of the institution, in society at large. And this means, first of all taking ourselves seriously: recognising that central responsibility of a woman to herself, without which we remain always the Other, the defined, the object, the victim; believing that there is a unique quality of validation, affirmation, challenge, support that one woman can offer another. Believing in the value and significance of women's experience, traditions, perceptions. Thinking of ourselves seriously, not as one of the boys, not as neuters, or androgynes, but as women.[25]

This is not so easy of course, because men are quite properly challenged by what we have to say, and for the majority of women who are in relationships with men, the difficult business of renegotiating the terms of those relationships has to take place if women are to be taken seriously.

At one level what men think shouldn't be important and it shouldn't alter what happens between women, but of course at another level it does matter to millions of women and whilst total separation is a necessary, valid and highly attractive political act, as well as an individual strategy for survival, if this Movement is to touch all women's lives then we must take their (those women's) considerations seriously and that means that all the revealing, re-defining and re-building must strengthen us to confront our relationships with men and alter them.[26]

Patricia De Wolfe summarises two contradictions arising out of Women's Studies courses from a student's point of view.

The first is that feminist theory will be hived off into Women's Studies options, leaving unchallenged the bulk of 'knowledge' produced by academics and presented to students. Women's Studies thus runs the risk of becoming another quirky subsection of sociology, rather than a radical challenge to the whole of patriarchal learning. The second danger is that Women's Studies will become increasingly remote from the Women's Movement. If such issues as the political implications of theory, the objectivity of academic standards, and the ways in which assessment creates hierarchies, are treated as unproblematic, feminists themselves may soon come to regard Women's Studies as irrelevant to the liberation of women, and as easily accommodated within the status quo.[27]

Issues relating to assessment do not of course apply in the context of non-vocational adult education classes, although the classes themselves are likely to be judged in terms of academic standards and theoretical soundness if the parent organisation is a university extramural department. But Women's Studies courses taught as internal university and college options are clearly highly subject to these contradictions. It seems strange to read in the American literature of 'minoring' and 'majoring' in Women's Studies, or to find discussed in the context of a course about lesbianism, whether or not the academic demands on students are sufficiently rigorous. Bonnie Zimmerman asks,

whether or not we are de-valuing ourselves and our students by lessening our standards. I assume we are teaching these courses because we have valuable information to share and ideas to investigate. It is essential to communicate to students the *indispensability* of knowledge, to convince them that knowledge is power. Possibly by holding to the serious design of these courses we will see our enrolments drop slightly, and we may alienate women to whom we have to give a C, but I think we will be faithful to both our academic and political goals.[28] (Zimmerman's italics)

This is exactly the dilemma that De Wolfe is talking about. The women's movement has always stressed the importance of every woman's experience and the values of collective learning. The emphasis is upon co-operation and not upon repeating hierarchical structures which, within patriarchy, are used to mystify expertise, bolster elitism and construct failure. Notions of assessment and the methods used to achieve it are based on competitive and individualistic values which have the effect of labelling some people competent and other useless. There has of course been a good deal of discussion about 'the objectivity' and 'effectiveness' of these procedures, but rather less about doing away with them altogether. Without grading and assessment the education system would look very different, and no sex or class or race would be able to monopolise success within it in quite the same way as now. Conventional assessment procedures in colleges and university courses reward those who can write examination essays logically, concisely and 'objectively' — none of which seem particularly appropriate yardsticks for evaluating a process of collective and reflective study, in which the inspiration of ideas, the sharing of experience, the construction of theory and the researching of evidence are likely to have been a group effort. 'Good academic standards' — even if these could be measured accurately — seem an inappropriate criterion to apply to a process which is not simply the study of a new subject area, but a reflection upon the selection and creation of knowledge generally, and a form of political action against the social oppression of women. The competitive individualism of grading and assessment inevitably divides students and reinforces the hierarchical relations between those regarded as teachers and assessors and those regarded as students. The subject content may be different, but the arrangements are exactly those which replicate patriarchal education and capitalist patriarchy.

Another problem is that so long as feminist perspectives on

history, culture, economics, sexuality, and the like, can be hived off into an option called Women's Studies, the broader implications of feminist objections to patriarchal knowledge and the construction of male superiority within the education system can be deflected. Women's Studies may be viewed as a kind of corrective to the theory and practice of the rest of the education system, but is unlikely to challenge firmly entrenched ideas about knowledge, intelligence and human experience, by remaining pigeon-holed as a minor option in a major degree — the rest of which remains unchanged.

Mary Evans[29] is not convinced by these arguments. She claims that Women's Studies is by definition a challenge to male intellectual hegemony, and has made significant contributions to the redefinition of patriarchal theories and forms of knowledge. Perhaps it is too soon to measure the permanence of these achievements, but the struggle for resources will have to be taken into account. As resources become less available, so the problems of permanence will increase. In stringent circumstances new courses, and especially those which are departures from tradition, and not of immediate use to industry, have greater difficulty in establishing themselves. Notions of affirmative action do not obtain in Britain, and seem increasingly ephemeral in the United States. In an atmosphere of recession and conservative administration at a national level, encouragement to the academy to shed its liberal/subversive elements are familiar experiences on both sides of the Atlantic. Potential rebels can be kept in control by keeping them in competition with each other for scarce resources so that Black Studies, Women's Studies and Adult Education Extension Studies may well find themselves arguing against each other for the same small slice of cake.

In these conditions the pressure to be legitimate and respectable in the terms of the academy is enormous. Identifying with women is a risky business professionally — contempt for women, although lightly disguised, remains rampant.

To reduce the risk to manageable proportions we try to make our work as safe as possible. In short our situation forces us to make our revolution respectable. The distortions this causes are many. It leads us to focus on 'safe' topics: it encourages us to try to import our new topics and contents in the same old forms; it makes us avoid using strong language — liberation, oppression, gynophobia, lesbian, radical feminist, and even women, which is nervously tucked into women and men . . . We are caught in a position when we keep trying to contribute to building a world in which the vocation of women no longer is the pleasing of men, by producing scholarship about women which will be pleasing to men.[30]

For reasons like these there is a good deal of disagreement among feminists about whether the concern to be taken seriously is also to lose touch with visions of a fundamentally different reality from the one which predominates in academia, and which decides what constitutes 'academic respectability'. The view that 'clever women can learn the rules and beat men at their own game' is little comfort if, in the process, feminism as a theory and a practice becomes the loser. If part of the success of winning is that we teach women to behave like men, we not only reproduce students according to the conventional requirements of patriarchy, but risk the further separation of 'educated' feminists (or will they be educated academics in feminism?) from other women in the wider community.

Maralyn Frye, after ten years of Women's Studies in the United States, describes some of the consequences of 'working within' the academy in an attempt to reform it from the inside. The decision to work from within, she claims, becomes almost irrevocable. The hard work involved in getting courses accepted, funded and protected demands considerable energy. Success means learning to operate the system, knowing about the power structure, finding your way around the administration, wheeling and dealing in the internal politics of departments, faculties and finance committees.

> Even though the increase in our power is frustratingly small, it is, in the meagre economy of the lives of women, a very significant reward and magnet, inviting us to remain where we are, and encouraging identification with the academy. These bonds which wed us to the academy, wed us to the decision to stay within it, and wed us to the other contradictions inherent in the situation.[31]

These are also the dilemmas discussed by Mary Evans. She summarises the main feminist reservations about Women' Studies as, either an exploitation or the de-radicalization (or both) of feminism and the Women's Movement. By becoming part of what is essentially an élitist and essentially male system of Higher Education, it is argued that those who teach (and presumably also those who study) Women's Studies also serve their own professional interests, and those of patriarchy, and the male ruling class. The energies that should be directed towards the transformation of social and sexual relationships are, it is suggested, dissipated in narrow scholastic battles which serve only to perpetuate those hierarchies of control and authority to which the Women's Movement is opposed.[32]

She feels, however, that the implicit resistance to Women's Studies is so great that it is unlikely that it will betray its fundamental allegiances. The challenge to patriarchy has to take place on many fronts — in the academy just as importantly as outside — to challenge male academic hegemony and to ensure 'that knowledge, itself a form of social power, is not produced solely in the interests of the powerful and the influential, to the detriment of the powerless and the weak.'[33]

Maralyn Frye's conclusions are somewhat different. She argues that in America, at least, Women's Studies courses have not been outrageous or radical enough, and that if students 'will not merely just follow us but will transcend us and our work . . . an important thing they must learn from us is that we cannot do what we must within institutions.'[34] So far as adult education provision is concerned, a new response to the liberated expectations of white, mostly middle-class women, is undoubtedly preferable to an adult education curriculum based on notions of female deficit or domesticity, but it is unlikely to appeal to black and working-class women in any significant way. Translated into elitist or narrowly instrumental educational activities, 'bourgeois feminism' incorporated within conventional education remains inaccessible and possibly even repellent to the majority of women.[35]

So long as feminism is generally associated with being middle class, white, educated and young, and Women's Studies does nothing to remove and redefine these categories and place them squarely in relation to the real conditions and economic situation which women face as a class of people, then in both educational and political terms we still have a long way to travel.

The problem is more serious than the continued exclusion of

black and working-class women from an education system which has traditionally excluded them might at first appear. It is also more serious than the failure to challenge the educational principles of patriarchal institutions — crucial though this struggle is. The separation of different groups of women from each other prevents the identification of common grievances and the recognition of shared subordination which needs to be our priority if the social stranglehold of patriarchy is to be confronted and resisted.

Notes

1. Otto Rank, *Beyond Psychology*, Dover, 1958.
2. Dale Spender (ed.) See *Men's Studies Modified*, Pergamon Press, 1981.
3. Barbara Ehrenreich and Deirdre English, *For Her Own Good. 150 Years of the Experts' Advice to Women*, Doubleday & Co., Anchor Press, 1978.
4. Adrienne Rich, 'Towards a Woman-centred University', in *On Lies, Secrets and Silence; Selected Prose 1966–78*, Virago, 1980.
5. Minnie Bruce Pratt, 'Rebellion', *Feminary*, vol. XI, nos. 1 and 2.
6. Jan Bradshaw, Wendy Davies and Patricia de Wolfe, *Women's Studies Courses in the UK*, Women's Research and Resources Centre Publication.
7. Mary Evans, 'In Praise of Theory: The Case for Women's Studies', *Feminist Review*, spring, 1982.
8. *Women, Class and Adult Education*, University of Southampton, 1981.
9. Mary Daly, *Beyond God the Father*, Beacon, 1973.
10. Adrienne Rich, 'Towards a Woman-centred University'.
11. Phyllis Chesler, 'Marriage and Psychotherapy', in Radical Therapist Collective (eds) *The Radical Therapist*, Ballantyne, 1971.
12. Don Zimmerman and Candace West, 'Sex Roles, Interruptions and Silences in Conversation', in Thorne and Henley (eds) *Language and Sex: Difference and Dominance*, Newbury House, 1975.
13. Pamela Fishman, 'Interactional Shitwork', *Heresies: A Feminist Publication on Arts and Politics*, May 1977.
14. Dale Spender, *Invisible Women: The Schooling Scandal*, Writers and Readers Publishing Co-operative Society, 1982.
15. Adrienne Rich, 'Taking Women Students Seriously', in *On Lies, Secrets and Silence*.
16. Spender, *Invisible Women*.
17. Lillian Faderman *Surpassing the Love of Men*, Junction Books.
18. Judith Mullard, personal communication.
19. Dale Spender, 'A Very Different Model of Adult Education', in *Women and Adult Education: Learning New Roles for a Changing World*, European Bureau of Adult Education, 1981.
20. Ibid.
21. Judith Mullard, personal communication.
22. Keith Jackson, Foreword to Jane L. Thompson (ed.) *Adult Education for a Change*, Hutchinson, 1980.
23. Marilyn French, *The Women's Room*, Sphere, 1978.
24. Paulo Freire, *Pedagogy of the Oppressed and Cultural Action for Freedom*, Penguin, 1972.

25. Adrienne Rich, 'Taking Women Students Seriously', in *On Lies, Secrets and Silence*.

26. Judith Mullard, personal communication.

27. Patricia de Wolfe, 'Women's Studies: The Contradictions for Students', in Dale Spender and Elizabeth Sarah (eds) *Learning to Lose*, The Women's Press, 1980.

28. Bonnie Zimmerman, 'Lesbianism 101', *Radical Teacher*, 17 November 1980.

29. Mary Evans, *In Praise of Theory*.

30. Maralyn Frye, 'On Second Thought . . .', *Radical Teacher*, 17.

31. Ibid.

32. Mary Evans, *In Praise of Theory*.

33. Ibid.

34. Maralyn Frye, 'On Second Thought . . .'

35. See page 26.

9 WOMEN'S EDUCATION AND RADICAL POLITICS

Pam Annas,[1] after more than a decade of intense work during which time Women's Studies has made the transition from 'a precarious to a permanent marginality', voices some of the questions which need to be worked through in future developments. Women's Studies, which began as 'a flash of vision' and with an examination of the evils and gross distortions of patriarchy, now needs to concentrate increasingly on the differences between us as women which have divided us under patriarchy, and which cannot be allowed to continue to divide us as feminists.

The divisions, of course, are based upon class, race, age, politics and sexual identity, and of these, class, race and sexual identity are perhaps the most urgent in our immediate struggle. Feminists who are also black, working class and lesbian (or all three) have been as concerned as any other group to establish their own identity and to reclaim their own realities as women. But the women's movement, dominated in both Britain and America by white, heterosexual, middle-class women, has not always been sufficiently sensitive to the issues which divide and potentially destroy us. And Women's Studies courses have not reflected sufficiently the material conditions and cultural inheritance of black, working-class or lesbian women.

The last two or three years has seen the re-emergence of 'consciousness raising' groups in the United States concerned especially with racism in the women's movement and the theme of the 1981 National Women's Studies Association (NWSA) annual conference was 'Women Respond to Racism'. The black feminist movement has begun to show its strength and this was reflected in the late 1970s by the emergency of Black Women's Studies. The publication of *This Bridge Called My Back: Writings by Radical Women of Color* in 1981 and *All Women are White, All the Blacks are Men, But Some of Us are Brave: Black Women's Studies* in 1982 are testimonies to this advance.

Afro-American, Native American, Hispanic, Asian American, Latina — all women of colour in the United States — have a common struggle. They live their lives at the point at which racism and sexism intersect, and since many are also extremely poor, they

128

are subject to capitalist class oppression too. Because black women are 'at the bottom'[2] they have no alternative but to 'fight the world' but 'If Black women were free, it would mean that everyone else would have to be free since (their) freedom would necessitate the destruction of all systems of oppression.'[3]

Statistics are hardly necessary to document what is painfully obvious — black women live and work in the poorest of circumstances, and are scarcely freer now from the racism of white America than they have ever been. Black women college graduates have moved into those occupations only which have been traditionally 'open' to them — teaching, social work and nursing. Yet only 5 per cent of black women who work are teachers; 19 per cent are nurses, 5 per cent are social workers, 3 per cent are health technicians. Only 1.1 per cent are employed as instructors, professors or college presidents (mostly in Bennett — a black women's college), 0.1 per cent are lawyers and judges, and only 0.3 per cent are doctors and surgeons. It does not take much imagination to appreciate where all the others are employed.

If the culture and intellect of white women have been discredited by patriarchy, blackness is classed as an additional 'affliction'. To claim a literary tradition and to affirm intellectual integrity — to exist positively — as a black woman in American (and British) society is to stand in direct opposition to most of that which passes for culture and ideas in the white academy. Black women bear the stigma of 'thinking like a woman' and 'acting like a nigger', in addition to the white prejudice which assumes that all blacks, collectively as a race, are congenitally deficient. Black characters have been repeatedly portrayed in white literature in extremely negative ways — as idle, illiterate and idiotic. White social science has depicted them as 'problems' caught up within a culture of 'poverty' and a 'cycle of cultural deprivation'; pathologically guilty as 'matriarchs' for emasculating shiftless lazy males, and for consigning fresh generations of ill-educated and ill-disciplined children to permanent psychological and social maladjustment.[4]

Liberal attempts to confront these stereotypes and explode the racist and sexist myths on which they are based has led to the development in recent years — of 'the life and times of prominent blacks' approach.[5] But the 'discovery' of key black figures and the demonstration of their courage and vision does little to remove the racist and sexist way in which the majority of black women are and have been viewed historically. To concentrate on prominent, and often highly educated, black women attributes no significance to the lives of working-class and poor women, and leave unquestioned the social circumstances which have permitted so few black women to be allowed to achieve prominence.

As with white women, the recording of history has been highly selective, and has concentrated in its accounts of black experience on men. Most of the images have been negative, but those applauding the abolition of slavery have depicted heroism as an essentially male quality. The fugitive slave, the fiery orator, the political activist, the abolitionist are, with the exception of Harriet Tubman and Sojourner Truth, always depicted as men. Black literary history is the same: 'Black women are ignored, trivialised, subordinated to men and effectively rendered invisible'.[6] Mary Helen Washington tells a different story.

> The articulation of a Black and female sub-culture is to be found in the early political writings of Black women educators and orators and abolitionists; in the collected and uncollected narratives of Black slave women; in the religious conversion narratives of Black women; in the folklore passed on from mother to daughter.'[7]

Pieced together, it becomes possible to construct a different literary tradition in which social, political and moral causes are most frequently the life and death issues which have encouraged women to write and to fight against oppression.

Unlike white women writers, 'constrained by the image of a beautiful and frail feminine object' or 'trapped by the neurotic strategies of the angel-in-the-home or the madwoman-in-the-attic', black women were not defined 'as women' in the same way by white patriarchy and consequently wrote from a different oppression — slavery. 'Those Black women who wrote did so to confront the evils of slavery, or to protest the lack of education and opportunity, or to condemn the ways racism and sexism impinged on their lives.'[8] The tradition lives on in the Blues of Bessie Smith, for example, whose comments on domestic economy in the 1920s speak for themselves:

> I've had a man for fifteen years
> Give him some room and his board.
> Once he was like a Cadillac
> Now he's an old worn-out Ford.

He never brought me a lousy dime
And put it in my hand.
Oh, there'll be some changes from now on
According to my plan.

He's got to get it, bring it, and put it right here
Or else he's gonna keep it out there.
If he must steal it, beg it, or borrow it somewhere
Long as he gets it, I don't care.

I'm tired of buying pork chops to grease his fat lips
And he'll have to find another place to park his ole hips
He's got to get it, and bring it, and put it right here
Or else he's gonna keep it out there.

The bee gets the honey and brings it to the comb
Else he's kicked out of his home-sweet-home
To show you that they brings it watch the dog and the cat
Everything even brings it, from a mule to a gnat.

The rooster gets the worm and brings it to the hen
That ought to be tip to all of you no-good men.
The ground hog even brings it and puts it in his hole
So my man has got to bring it, doggone his soul.

He's got to get it, and bring it, and put it right here
Or else he's gonna keep it out there.
He can steal it, beg it, or borrow it somewhere
Long as he gets it, chile, I don't care.

I'm gonna tell him like the chinaman when you don't
  bring-um check
You don't get-um laundry if you wring-um damn neck.
You got to get it, and bring it, and put it right here
Or else you're gonna keep it out there.

By the 1960s Nina Simone took the offensive against racism and performed 'Old Jim Crow' and 'Backlash Blues' to white audiences who knew they were under attack, and to black audiences who were getting organised. There was no compromise when she told white America:

> Oh this white country's full of lies
> Y'all gonna die and die like flies
> I don't trust you anymore
> When you keep saying 'Go slow'.
>
> But that's just the trouble — too slow
> Desegregation, mass participation, unification — too slow
> Do things gradually and bring more tragedy.
>
> You don't have to live next door to me
> Just leave me my equality.

The tradition lives on in the writings of Zora Neale Hurston, Margaret Walker, Toni Morrison and Alice Walker; in Toni Cade Bambara, Audre Lorde, Pat Parker and Ann Allen Shockley. But ironically it is as oddities — insignificant or fleetingly fashionable — that they are most frequently measured by white critics. Barbara Smith, in an excellent contribution to *But Some of Us are Brave*, reveals how Sara Blackburn of the *New York Times* displayed her lack of understanding and her racism in her review of Toni Morrison's novel, Sula, in 1973:

> Toni Morrison is far too talented to remain only a marvellous recorder of the black side of American provincial life. If she is to maintain the large and serious audience she deserves, she is going to have to address a riskier contemporary reality than this beautiful but none the less distanced novel. And if she does this, it seems to me that she might easily transcend that early and unintentionally limiting classification 'black woman writer' and take her place among the most serious, important and talented American novelists now working.

Smith comments,

> Recognising Morrison's exquisite gift, Blackburn unashamedly asserts that Morrison is 'too talented' to deal with mere Black folk, particularly those double nonentities Black women. In order to be accepted as 'serious', 'important', 'talented' and 'American', she must obviously focus her efforts upon chronicling the doings of white men.[9]

The extent to which white feminists can still 'be surprised' by black talent; can fail to understand that the experience of racism means that sexism is only a part of multiple oppression, and can take refuge in guilt as an excuse for ignorance and inaction, are some measure of the work we still have to do. Adrienne Rich, addressing the 4th NWSA conference in Storrs, Connecticut, said,

> It seems to me that the word guilt has arisen too often in discussions like these. Women of color in their anger are charged with provoking guilt in white women. White women accuse each other of provoking guilt. It is guilt endlessly that is supposed to stand between white women and disobedience, white women and true rebellion. I have come to wonder whether guilt, with its attendant connotations of being emotionally overwhelmed and bullied or paralysed, is not more a form of defensive resentment or self-protection than an authentic response to the past and its warts. Guilt does not move. Guilt does not look you in the eye. Guilt does not speak a personal language. I would like to ask every white woman who feels that her guilt is being provoked in discussions of racism, to consider what use she has for this guilt? and how it uses her? and to decide for herself if a guilt-ridden feminism, a guilt-ridden rebellion, sounds like a viable way of life?

Audre Lorde is even more explicit:

> We are not as women examining racism in a political and social vacuum. We operate in the teeth of a system for whom racism and sexism are primary, established, necessary props of profit . . . I am a lesbian woman of color whose children eat regularly because I work in a university. If their full bellies make me fail to recognise my communality with a woman of color whose children do not eat, because she can't find work; or a woman who has no children because her insides are rotten from home abortions and sterilisation; if I fail to recognise the lesbian who chooses not to have children, or the woman who remains closeted because her homophobic community is her only life support; the woman who chooses silence instead of another death; the woman who is terrified lest my anger triggers the explosion of hers; if I fail to recognise these women as other faces of myself, then I am contributing to each of their oppressions, but also to my own.

> I am not free while any woman is unfree, even when her shackles are very different from my own. And I am not free as long as any one person of color remains chained — nor are you.

In Britain the links between sexism and racism have been made even less perfectly. I have been to countless meetings in which white women who are part of a movement concerned with the conditions of all women say 'it's hard to discuss racism because no black women come to the classes' or the other side of the coin, 'I don't think I'm really qualified to talk about it'. In other words, racism is a black woman's problem and only black women can discuss it. The curriculum of Women's Studies remains essentially race-blind and our movement is diminished accordingly.

In Britain too discussions about sexuality are less evident than in the United States. They come shrouded in psychological mystification and surface in abstracted debates about 'the politics of patriarchal knowledge' versus the 6th demand of the Women's Liberation Movement.[10] Lesbian experience figures rarely in the content of Women's Studies courses. It may be a part of the hidden curriculum in that Women's Studies frequently promote a closeness between those involved which can include sexual attraction and admiration, and because a common experience of the women's movement has been the joy with which women, liberated from male definitions of our sexuality, have discovered our capacity to love each other physically as well as emotionally.[11] But subject matter explicitly concerned with lesbian existence and lesbian culture is conspicuous by its absence. There are a number of reasons for this.

Patriarchy has done its job very well. The general assumption it has created is that women are innately attracted to men sexually, and that heterosexual relationships are the relationships which most normal people choose naturally. These assumptions persist despite many women's experience of dissatisfaction, revulsion and fear in 'normal' heterosexual relationships. These assumptions persist despite evidence that men in all societies and at all periods of history have acted as pimps, procurers, traffickers in sexual slavery, owners of brothels, purveyors of pornography, managers of prostitution, wife-beaters, child-molesters, incest-perpetrators, and rapists.[12] And that women, economically and socially dependent on men, have been the instruments and victims of sexual abuse, sexual humiliation and sexual violence — the luckless recipients of the less romantic face of heterosexual love.

Compared to these 'natural' manifestations of 'normal' hetero-sexual relationships, sensuality between women, loving and passionate friendships, lifelong commitments as co-workers, lovers, comrades and friends are considered sick and queer and perverse. Some writers[13] have explained the widespread social revulsion at the idea of lesbian love as an indication of men's fear and hatred of women. But of course love between women and women who make their primary commitment to women who are supremely challenging to patriarchy, for their action implies women's capacity to be indifferent to men altogether, and also the denial of automatic rights to women's bodies, minds and gratuitous labour.

Heterosexuality, therefore, is an institution which patriarchy has a profound vested interest in maintaining and promoting. Historically this has been done by force and violence when necessary, and by persistent indoctrination and ideological blockading as a matter of course. The whole apparatus of romantic love reinforced by commercial and cultural arrangements has seen so that.

Women, economically and socially dependent upon men, learn from an early age that it is natural to see men as the creators and confirmers of their sexual happiness and fulfilment. This also implies a slave-like submission to male supremacy at the expense of female solidarity. It means,

Internalizing the values of the coloniser and actively partici-pating in carrying out the colonisation of one's self and one's sex . . . Male identification is the act whereby women place men above women, including themselves, in credibility, status, and importance in most situations, regardless of the comparative quality the women may bring to the situation . . . Interaction with women is seen as a lesser form of relating at every level.[14]

For women to resist the coercive nature of compulsory hetero-sexuality is not easy. Lesbian existence has been ignored, deleted and discredited historically. Lesbian love has been punished by death in some circumstances, and repeatedly diagnosed by 'experts' as a disease. To accept, just as capitalism or racism are man-made social and political institutions that thrive on coercion and false consciousness to survive, that compulsory heterosexuality — a creation of patriarchy — also has to be contrived, imposed and managed, is an electrifying shock to those trained to assume that sexual preference is innate.

Discussions within the women's movement have had to face this most profound of issues. But as with other revelations, it emerges that we are not the first to arrive at the same conclusion. Lesbian women have been declaring and demonstrating and living their love for women throughout recorded time, but in a hostile world in which women are not supposed to survive except in relation with and in service to men, entire communities of women have simply been erased from the history books. Their letters, diaries and memories have been burned and destroyed[15] as men, anxious to suppress, and women fearful of the homophobic communities in which they lived, have colluded to represent the semblance of heterosexual priority.

It has proved impossible to completely destroy the truth however, although its significance has frequently been misrepresented or ignored. Lillian Faderman[16] has produced a magnificent testament to the power and commitment of love between women throughout five centuries in western Europe and America. She illustrates how romantic friendships between women in the seventeenth, eighteenth, and nineteenth centuries not only sustained great support and intimacy, but were also inspirational in a cultural and creative sense. So long as these friendships could be seen by men as 'feminine . . . as an activity in which women indulged when men were unavailable, or as an apprenticeship, or appetite whetter to heterosexual sex'[17] they were generally condoned, but transvestite women, and those who demanded masculine liberties and privileges, were persecuted and sometimes even executed. By the end of the nineteenth century and the beginning of the twentieth, under pressure from feminism and increasing demands by women for social equality with men, women who identified with women became more of a threat to patriarchal omnipotence. Sexologists like Kraft-Ebing, Freud, Hirschfield and Havelock Ellis — all men — helped to define lesbian love as a medical problem, and its victims as inverted, twisted, sick and tortured creatures.

> For many of them, without models to show that love between women was not intrinsically wrong or unhealthy, the experts pronouncements about lesbianism worked as a self-fulfilling prophecy. They became as confused and tormented as they were supposed to be.[18]

Not until the 1970s have women rediscovered the power of love between women as something other than a deviance or a retreat in fear from men, but a positive, powerful, chosen preference, with a heritage and a future. The possibility of love between women after all promises the prospect of relationships which are qualitatively different and — given the oppressive nature of male–female relationships — qualitatively superior to those between men and women. They represent an ultimate affirmation of friendship, of identification and of commitment in a political sense as well as an emotional sense. They offer the possibility of the genuine re-creation of identity and relationship beyond the restrictions of patriarchal definitions.

For all of these reasons both men and women have cause to be fearful: men because such a possibility undermines their power, and women because a lifetime of conditioning to the contrary has to be re-examined, and because to stand as a lesbian in a grossly homophobic society is an act of supreme courage.

Black women in the academy who are able and prepared to teach Black Women's Studies are few. They are the last to be hired and the first to be fired. Gloria Hull and Barbara Smith note that,

despite popular myths about being 'double tokens', our salaries, promotions, tenure and general level of acceptance in the white male 'community of scholars' are all quite grim. The current backlash against affirmative action is also disastrous for Black women workers, including College teachers. And of course the fact that a course in Black Lesbian Studies has, to our knowledge, yet to be taught, has absolutely nothing to do with the 'nonexistence' of Black lesbian experience but everything to do with fear and refusal to acknowledge that this experience does in fact exist.[19]

White women's position in British post-school education and American universities is only marginally more secure, and schooled within the values and according to the rules of patriarchy, women scholars, for their own survival, have frequently adopted the language, values and behaviour patterns prescribed by the institutions in which they work. To do otherwise would also be to risk tenure, job security and allegations of illogical, emotional, incompetent — and thus unscholarly — behaviour. The choice of teaching materials, subject matter and research topics which are informed or enhanced by the personal experience of being a woman, risk allegations of being tendentious or not sufficiently academic, and contribute to the barely disguised conviction that, apart from being 'interesting' in a liberal–pluralistic sense, Women's Studies, taught by feminist teachers, are unprofessional, dilletante and not to be taken too seriously. To attach the label 'lesbian' to these pursuits would intensify the resistance enormously. This is not to say that feminist academics have not engaged in the clarification of this repression and increasingly refused to be silenced, but there are as yet few examples — in Britain anyway — of courses dealing in an uncompromising way with female sexuality and lesbian existence.

In California the notorious Briggs initiative, calling for the dismissal of any teacher advocating homosexuality, makes clear that homophobia is alive and well in America society also — a fear and hatred well cultivated by the activities of the Moral Majority, concerned to purge American society of its unpatriotic dissidents, communists and perverts. Despite the professional risks, courses about lesbian experience and culture have begun to be taught in a number of US colleges and universities, and lesbian–feminist scholarship is becoming increasingly visible in subject caucuses, conferences and publications.

The majority of teachers on both sides of the Atlantic still define reference to lesbian experience out of their classrooms, however, and rationalise the omission in terms of students' intolerance — 'my students have a hard enough time with feminism as it is'. For those working with working-class women the assumption is even stronger that, working-class lesbians notwithstanding, lesbian identification will be 'the kiss of death' to any continuation of learning. This is sad really — especially since — as Adrienne Rich makes clear

Woman identification is *a source of energy, a potential spring-head of female power*, violently curtailed and wasted under the institution of heterosexuality. The denial of reality and visibility to women's passion for women, women's choice of women as allies, life companions and community; the forcing of such relationships into dissimulation and their disintegration under intense pressure has meant an incalculable loss to the power of all women to change the social relations of the sexes, and to liberate ourselves and each other.[20] (Rich's italics)

The women's movement may have been more successful in making theoretical links with the concerns of working-class women. Most feminists are also socialists, and many have come to feminism originally through a political and intellectual commitment to socialism. The nature of class oppression is well understood intellectually, and part of the radical reconstruction of knowledge which until recently has been 'hidden from history' has focused on working-class experience as well as women's lives in general. The republication of letters and diaries written by working-class women in the Women's Co-operative guilds[21] for example, has demonstrated the concern about working-class women's lives, and publications like *One Hand Tied Behind Us*[22] has served to remind us that the struggle for the vote in Britain was not simply the pre-occupation of bored middle-class housewives and charismatic cult figures. The tools of oral history have been developed powerfully to record the lived experiences of women as domestic and industrial workers[23] and some attempt has been made to re-examine trade union history in search of women's contribution and experience.[24]

There is little room for complacency however. When Evelyn Tension — a working-class woman from the East End of London — joined the Women's Liberation Movement she met intellectual Marxists and radical feminists for the first time. '*I* was who they were talking about, but I didn't understand a word they said.'[25] Others have fled in confusion and alienation from similar encounters.

> They all seemed so young — crowded round with their roll-ups and pints of bitter — peering through little round glasses and talking about blokes I'd never heard of — Engels and Gramsci and all that lot.

> When we got home, me and Ann would sit up half the night and she'd explain to me everything they'd been saying — in English!

> When I joined I was quite a novelty I suppose, I was 45, with six kids, living on an estate — a *real* woman. Mind you, the novelty soon wore off, and nobody offered to give me a lift home when they roared off in their cars at the end of the meeting.

So long as working-class women feel this degree of intimidation and this degree of alienation, we have problems.

A scholarly or romantic interest in working-class culture is not enough. As Paul Willis makes clear, 'Working-class culture is generally not one of celebration and mastery. It is basically one of compromise and settlement: a creative attempt to make the best of hard and brutalising conditions.'[26] We have seen how, for working-class girls, the culture of femininity is a conscious response to the meaningless of school — and is in itself an unlikely liberation from either capitalist or sexual oppression.[27] Groomed for marriage but thrown temporarily into mundane, repetitive, unskilled work, the expectation of a better life beyond the factory is still, for young working-class women, shrouded in dreams. Anna Pollert describes Churchman's tobacco factory in Bristol:

> The dreams of escape were cushioned in a feminine culture as the girls tried to 'feminise' the ruthless atmosphere of the production line. Romance permeated the factory. The glowingly lipsticked magazine covers, the love stories, the male pop heroes, the pictures of boyfriends, the circulation of wedding photographs, all were a bizarre contrast to the racket of the dark oily machines. I was frequently caught out by the convention of rings: signet rings, friendship rings, eternity rings — to be distinguished from the high status of the engagement ring, next only to the pure golden sheen of the wedding ring. Femininity and attractiveness were endlessly discussed: fashion, hair, skin, bodies, diets, slimming. One girl spent a third of her wages on a slimming course at a health and beauty studio. Then, personal life, relationships and feelings, 'courting' and marriage — fidelity and infidelity, freedom and possessiveness — all were discussed.[28]

Of course working-class men are also diminished by factory work:

> You move from one boring, dirty, monotonous job to another boring, dirty, monotonous job. And then to another boring, dirty, monotonous job. And somehow you're supposed to come out of it all 'enriched'. But I never feel 'enriched' — I just feel knackered.
> Even when you're at home you see these fucking green bags. Just lie back and shut your eyes and all you see is green.[29]

As breadwinners and shiftworkers men become cut off from their

families, and the necessity of hard, endless, gruelling work is a poor
substitute for leisure and family enjoyment.

But for women,

> The privatised family becomes their cage, the men their
> overlords. As they continue in wage labour, their exploitation
> becomes shaped by this oppression. As the dreams of romance
> and marriage as escapes imperceptibly transform into the double
> burden of work, their lives become crushed and split at the same
> time, between home and workplace, reproduction and social
> production, domestic labour and wage labour . . . They serve
> two masters — the employers and the husband — sometimes
> three, if you include their 'brothers' in the trade union. And so,
> from having started in unskilled work self-deprecatingly, now
> contradictions — and guilt, always guilt — take over. In the
> meantime, wage labour, which seemed temporary, becomes
> peripheral instead, perpetuating poor organisation, exploitation
> — in short, second rate 'women's work'.[30]

For women without choice at work and without resources to ease
the struggle at home the double shift of industry and domestic
labour continues unabated. At Churchman's Pollert found that,

> The daily routine of most women began around 5.30 to 6 a.m. to
> 'do a bit of work'. They then had to catch the bus and often wait
> for half an hour in case they missed it. Work started at 7.30 a.m.
> prompt, but rather than risk being late many got in at 7 a.m. for
> 'a cup of tea and a fag'. At 9.30 a.m. there was a fifteen minute
> break for a quick bite and a cup of coffee. Lunch was between
> 12.30 p.m. and 1.30 p.m., during which some stayed in the
> canteen, but many went over to the Bedminster to do some shop-
> ping. Work 'finished' at 4.30 p.m., but of course started again.
> They shopped, caught the bus, got home, had a quick cup of tea,
> cooked the tea and did more housework. It was quite normal to
> have less than an hour's 'free time', perhaps to watch television,
> before going to bed ready to get up next day — and start again,
> the same old pattern.[31]

However 'knackered' and resentful working-class men might be —
'time off' has a meaning, there is the pub or football or friends.
'For working-class women there is no relief, no escape. A break

from wage-work merely brings them face to face with another pile of work at home.'[32]

Pollert's picture of the Bristol factory is not all without possibility however. She describes also resistance, a struggle for dignity and control, and the collective strength which develops from shared experience and mutual support. Together at work women have the possibility to break out of the isolation that constrains women at home,

> They can build up confidence, share problems, have a laugh, learn collectively. From this experience they can build up a new consciousness, not only to fight against the abuses of female wage labour, but also the sexual oppression which cuts right across the home and the workplace.[33]

It is important to remember that events which coincided with, and influence, the re-emergence of feminism in Britain were the women machinists' equal pay strike at Ford's in Dagenham, the women's 'work in' at the leather factory in Fakenham, and the night cleaners' campaign for better pay and conditions in London. The emerging women's movement welcomed and supported these demonstrations of working women's anger. Subsequent industrial action by women at Trico, Electrolux, Grunwick's, Chix and Lee Jeans have also been rallying points for feminists keen to support and to endorse the links between women's struggles and class struggles.

But despite all of this, the women's movement remains an essentially middle-class movement, focusing on the personal, professional and domestic concerns of middle-class women. Many of those who have worked in Women's Aid, pregnancy and abortion advice services and Rape Crisis centres, have done so 'on behalf of' working-class women rather than alongside working-class women on unequal terms. The problem of class distance, patronage and 'unintentional' oppression are enormous. For this reason the

> movement has to be set in a wider context. Without digging to the roots of women's oppression in class society feminism is a futile belief system. Women's liberation has to embrace the ideas and strategies of a political movement committed to toppling capitalism.[34]

as well as confronting patriarchal systems of private and public control.

When it comes to Women's Studies courses, these contradictions are transported into the classroom. University education is by definition an elitist experience and, as we have seen, middle-class women are also most likely to be the majority of students in extramural and WEA adult education classes. The experience of involving community women in the Women's Studies programmes of American colleges and universities has also been equally fraught. But just as racism and homophobia cannot simply be dismissed as black or lesbian women's problems, neither can the general non-participation of working-class women in the 'official' women's movement and in Women's Studies courses be held to be a problem of 'working-class apathy' or 'down-trodden drudgery'.

Michele Russell describes a Women's Studies programme in Detroit. Twenty-two women turned up,

all on their way from somewhere to something . . . They have all been pregnant more than once and made various decisions about abortion, adoption, monogamy, custody and sterilisation. Some are great grandmothers. They are a cross section of hundreds of Black women I have known . . . We start where they are. We exchange stories of children's clothes ripped or lost, of having to go to school with sons and explain why Che is always late and how he got that funny name, anyway, to teachers who shouldn't have to ask and don't really care. They tell of waiting for men to come home from the night shift so they can get the money or car necessary to get downtown, or power failures in the neighbourhood, or administrative red tape at the college, or compulsory overtime on their own jobs, or the length of food stamp lines, or just being tired and needing sleep. Some of the stories are funny, some sad; some elicit outrage and praise from the group. It's a familiar and comfortable ritual in Black culture. It's called testifying.[35]

The role of the teacher? It is to make the process conscious and the content significant; not to stop at commiseration but to make generalisations and look for action. Nothing which can be discussed is too trivial for political analysis — it might be clothes, or 'the blues' or the shabby, unsatisfactory conditions that discussion groups like this usually have to put up with. It is important also to build upon the testimony of other working-class women. The words of Johnny Tillman — founder of the National Welfare Rights Organization in Watts — provide a good way in:

> I'm a woman. I'm a black woman. I'm a poor woman. I'm a fat woman. I'm a middle aged woman. And I'm on welfare.
>
> In this country if you're anyone of those things — poor, Black, fat, female, middle-aged, on welfare — you count less as a human being. If you're all of those things, you don't count at all, except as a statistic.
>
> I am a statistic. I am forty-five years old. I have raised six children. I grew up in Arkansas and I worked there for fifteen years in a laundry, making about twenty or thirty dollars a week, picking cotton on the side for carfare. I moved to California in 1959 and worked in a laundry there for nearly four years. In 1963, I got too sick to work anymore. My husband and I had split up. Friends helped me to go on welfare.
>
> They didn't call it welfare. They called it AFDC — Aid to Families With Dependent Children. Each month I get $363 for my kids and me. I pay $128 a month rent; $30 for utilities, which include gas, electricity and water; $120 for food and non-edible household essentials; $50 for school lunches for the three children in junior and senior high school who are not eligible for reduced cost meal progams. This leaves $5 per person per month for everything else — clothing, shoes, recreation, incidental personal expenses, and transportation. This cheque allows $1 a month for transportation a month for me, but none for my children. That's how we live.
>
> Welfare is all about dependency. It is the most prejudiced institution in this country, even more than marriage, which it tries to imitate.
>
> The truth that AFDC is like a super-sexist marriage. You trade in *a* man for *the* man. But you can't divorce him if he treats you bad. He can divorce you, of course, cut you off anytime he wants. But in that case, he keeps the kids, not you.
>
> *The* man runs everything. In ordinary marriage, sex is supposed to be for your husband. On AFDC you're not supposed to have any sex at all. You give up control of your own body. It's a condition of aid. You may even have to agree to get your tubes tied so you can never have more children, just to avoid being cut off welfare.

The man, the welfare system, controls your money. He tells you what to buy, what not to buy, where to buy it, and how much things cost. If things — rent for instance — really cost more than he says they do, it's just too bad for you. You've just got to make your money stretch.

The man can break into your home any time he wants to and poke into your things. You've got no right to protest. You've got no right to privacy. Like I said, welfare's a super-sexist marriage.[36]

A significant number of women know about life on welfare — many others know how close the experience of all working-class women is to life on the breadline: a divorce, an accident at work, unemployment, prolonged illness can mean the difference between life and death to anyone who lives without the security of economic independence. Learning has to make sense of these and other experiences rooted in class oppression if we are really serious about class consciousness, and about the possibilities of social action and political change.

There is of course no problem, or very little problem, so far as employers are concerned, when adult education tutors express solidarity with local civic societies, parent-teacher's associations, literacy students or the handicapped, but when welfare dependants, or lesbian mothers, or black women, conscious of their feminist interests, want to use the normal democratic procedures in society and bring them into the curriculum of adult education, then there are problems. It is when students who do not normally participate in adult education, for all the reasons we know about, can see the direct relationship between learning, action and their lives, that adult education begins to live up to its claims about 'relevance' and 'responsiveness to students' needs'. Ironically, it is frequently in just these circumstances that institutional constraints intended to preserve the demarcation between political theory and political action are intensified.

The problem for many middle-class, white feminists is to understand the difference between true and false rebellion. White capitalist patriarchy will allow a certain degree of argument and independent thought. 'Women's Lib' has matured and become incorporated into the language and superficial behaviour of most self-respecting liberal–socialists. A good many educated women have used the ideology of economic independence, job-sharing and role swapping to establish careers which bring satisfaction and economic rewards. Many have become 'lifestyle feminists'[37] with husbands and boyfriends who have cultivated the good-humoured acceptance of feminist ideas and who behave as non-oppressive, anti-sexist men, cooking the ratatouille, organising crèches at women's conferences and turning a blind eye to untidy houses and piles of dirty washing. This is not the experience of most working-class women.

In the academy, where a semblance of pluralism persists, it is perfectly acceptable to introduce elements of Women's Studies material into a curriculum which, during the last ten years or so, has also made space for Black Studies, the teaching of race relations, and working-class history. None of these has posed any particular threat to the hegemony of traditional disciplines and patterns of academic thought and women can be incorporated as easily as the rest.

In all of these circumstances women can wear their feminist hearts on their sleeves and the world will continue much the same. It is only when women refuse to toe the line, when we renounce the rewards of good behaviour and resist all attempts to be incorporated that true rebellion comes into its own. Only when women cross the line drawn by patriarchy, and when our collusion with racism, homophobia and class oppression can no longer be guaranteed, that real resistance and real possibilities for change begin to emerge.

Notes

1. In *Radical Teacher: A Newsjournal of Socialist Theory and Practice*, November 1980.

2. Michelle Wallace, 'A Black Feminist's Search for Sisterhood', in Gloria Hull, Patricia Bell Scott and Barbara Smith (eds) *All The Women are White, All the Blacks are Men, But Some of Us are Brave: Black Women's Studies*, The Feminist Press, 1982.

3. *'A Black Feminist Statement, The Combahee River Collective'*, ibid.

4. See Patricia Bell Scott, 'Debunking Sapphire: Towards a Non-Racist and Non-Sexist Social Science', ibid.

5. Ibid.

6. Marg Helen Washington, 'The Self Invented Woman: A Theoretical Framework for a Literary History of Black Women', *Radical Teacher*, November 1980.

7. Ibid.

8. Ibid.

9. Barbara Smith, 'Towards a Black Feminist Criticism', in Hull *et al.* (eds) *But Some of Us are Brave.*

10. I.e. an end to discrimination against lesbians and a woman's right to define her own sexuality.

11. See Anna Coote and Beatrix Campbell, *Sweet Freedom*, Picador, 1982.

12. Kathleen Barry, *Female Sexual Slavery*, quoted in Adrienne Rich, *Compulsory Heterosexuality and Lesbian Existence*, Onlywomen Press Ltd, 1981.

13. E.g. Karen Horney, H. R. Hayes, Wolfgang Lederer, Dorothy Dinnerstein.

14. Kathleen Barry, *Female Sexual Slavery*.

15. Adrienne Rich, *Compulsory Heterosexuality*.

16. Lillian Faderman, *Surpassing the Love of Men*, Junction Books, 1981.

17. Ibid.

18. Ibid.

19. Gloria Hull and Barbara Smith, 'The Politics of Black Women's Studies', in Hull *et al.* (eds) *But Some of Us are Brave*.

20. Adrienne Rich, *Compulsory Heterosexuality*.

21. Margaret Llewellyn Davies (ed.) *Life as We Have Known It, by Co-operative Working Women*, Virago, 1977.

22. Jill Liddington and Jill, Norris, *One Hand Tied Behind Us*, Virago, 1978.

23. See Women's History Issue, *Oral History, The Journal of the Oral History Society*, vol. 5, no. 2.

24. See e.g. Labour Research Dept, *Women in Trade Unions*, Allen & Unwin, 1919; Sheila Lewenhak, *Women and Trade Unions*, Ernest Benn Ltd, 1977; Sarah Boston, *Women Workers and the Trade Unions*, Davis-Poynter, 1980.

25. Evelyn Tension, *You Don't Need A Degree To Read The Writing On The Wall*, Catcall, January 1978.

26. Paul Willis, *Learning to Labour: How Working-class Kids Get Working-class Jobs*, Saxon House, 1978.

27. See Chapter 3.

28. Anna Pollert, *Girls, Wives, Factory Lives*, Macmillan, 1981.

29. Unskilled workers at 'Chemco' interviewed in Nicols and Beynon, *Living with Capitalism*, RKP, 1977.

30. Pollert, *Girls, Wives*.

31. Ibid.

32. Ibid.

33. Ibid.

34. Ibid.

35. Michele Russell, 'Black-Eyed Blues Connections: Teaching Black Women', in Hull *et al.* (eds) *But Some of Us are Brave*.

36. Johnny Tillman, written in 1965, quoted in ibid.

37. Barbara Ehrenreich, 'The Women's Movements: Feminist and Antifeminist', *Radical America*, vol. 15, nos. 1 and 2, spring 1981.

10 WORK IN PROGRESS — A REPORT FROM SOUTHAMPTON

I would like in this chapter to focus on a specific illustration of 'work in progress' in women's education in Southampton — not because I consider it to be particularly unique or any more worthy of attention than countless other Women's Studies developments in recent years, but as an illustration of practice which may be of interest to others concerned with women's educational programmes.

One of the traditional assumptions about reflection and analysis is that what is being examined has to be studied over a significant period of time so that the consistency of certain characteristics can be distinguished from those which are insignificant and superficial. It is also usual to include quantifiable data, gleaned from attitude tests, questionnaires, interviews and the like. The main problems of this approach, of course, are that in the process of identifying 'key variables' as distinct from 'marginal variables' a great deal of the significance of day-to-day developments can be dismissed as aberrations, or more frequently go unrecognised, and the complexity of profoundly important attitudinal and behavioural responses can get reduced mechanistically to a series of input–output measurements.

I prefer, therefore, to describe and explain what seem to me to be the significant elements of our work, including the comments of some of those who are involved in what we do, as together we have tried to take stock of our adventure. Hopefully our experience will prove useful, and provide debating points for others concerned to develop an alternative philosophy and practice from the ones which currently dominate adult education provision.

The Liberal Legacy

In 1973, in the wake of the government's poverty programme, the identification of Educational Priority Areas, Urban Aid and the National Community Development Project — all of them essentially British versions of America's 'war on poverty' launched during the liberal polemicism of the Kennedy–Johnson era — the Russell Committee published its *Plan for Development* in which, among other things, it encouraged adult education to align itself with others of the 'caring professions' to target 'the disadvantaged' as special priority groups in the provision of adult education. Non-formal education with groups who do not usually participate in institution-based adult education, and called within the boundaries of the Inner London Education Authority (ILEA), 'outreach work', was already well established in London by 1973; but with the seal of approval from Russell, other providing organisations in different parts of the country were encouraged to commit some of their resources to development work with so-called disadvantaged groups. The nebulous but popularly comprehensive term 'community education' became the umbrella beneath which a profusion of variously motivated, variously sponsored and variously committed projects made connections with neighbouthood groups engaged in everything from mother-and-toddlers meetings and toy libraries to trades councils and tenants' action groups.

In some of the better liaisons adult education workers committed to the political and cultural concerns of working-class people provided educational back-up and support in campaigns organised and controlled by community groups, and arranged for educational resources to be made more widely available to groups unaccustomed to finding adult education provision sensitive or responsive to their concerns.[1] Too often, however, the well-meaning enthusiasm of conscience-stricken liberals encouraged the proliferation of short-term, poorly funded, and frequently ill-conceived sorties into 'inner-city blackspots' and 'priority estates'[2] in association with others of the 'caring professions' — social services, probation and the church — to 'meet needs', to counsel and co-opt, and to engender 'community spirit' amongst those unsociable enough to display the 'many symptoms of individual, family and community malfunctioning'.[3]

This is not to suggest that some of the outcomes of such initiatives have not been useful, pleasurable or constructive for those engaged in them — especially when the professionals concerned were politically sensitive to the contradictions of their position as cultural-go-betweens, and have been prepared to align themselves with oppressed groups at the expense of professional loyalties.[4] But the recent history of non-formal education, outreach work, and community development is littered with the debris of raised expectations, unfulfilled promises and unread reports gathering dust on the shelves of those who have immersed themselves in and moved on to more fashionable investments.

The beginning of the women's education programme in Southampton in the mid-1970s was prey to this kind of thinking. Limited resources were made available for neighbourhood-based meetings and discussion groups for women. Single parents, prisoners' wives, council-estate mothers of pre-school children were identified as 'prime targets'. For development and research purposes the usual elitism of 'university-level' curriculum and pedagogy were suspended by a rationale that sought to legitimise non-formal education with 'disadvantaged' groups in terms of 'exploring the interface' between adult education and social work.[5] The assumptions underlying these developments were based on traditional and restricted views of women, and were more concerned with therapeutic control than the clarification of critical awareness. Some of the discussion leaders were men who, if they had understood anything about 'consciousness raising' among women, would have appreciated the unhelpful and inappropriate imposition of their presence. The importance of the education that was being offered was cloaked in informality, bring-and-buy sales, wishing wells,[6] cups of tea and children's outings. Education as such was scarcely mentioned, and was smuggled in by stealth in the patronising misconception that openly declared it would 'frighten off' potential 'clients'. Fortunately the interference of the university did little damage because very little came of all its efforts.

However, the commitment of resources to neighbourhood-based education with women had been established, and others of us were pleased to continue the tradition, albeit from a radically different perspective. We made use of the practices we had learned from the women's movement: of small, informal discussions in which the different experiences and perceptions and concerns of the group became the content of discussion and the base from which to explore, analyse, make generalisations and validate the knowledge being constructed and generated. Sometimes the meetings were focused on specific issues like housing, education or domestic violence. Sometimes themes like sex roles or welfare rights were pursued over a period of weeks. Several times we organised short courses about workers rights for women for whom a dispute at work and poor or non-existent union organisation encouraged them to seek out information.[7]

Important though all of these initiatives were, they had built-in limitations. The less liberal wing of our department dismissed the activities as remedial education and inappropriate concerns for a university to be engaged in. The more liberal wing became increasingly alarmed about the political ramifications of activities which were once associated with self-help and social skills, and were now being described in language which presumed a social class and feminist analysis of society in a way which challenged the complacency and limitations of liberal tolerance. More important was the scarcity of resources and on-going commitment to activities considered marginal to the 'real concerns' of the department. All the more so as small-scale, short-term neighbourhood initiatives repeatedly revealed women intelligent and hungry for knowledge, articulate, resourceful and real — women usually tossed out of school as 'failures' and generally unenthusiastic about what conventional adult education had to offer. To suggest — as some colleagues did — that having been 'caught' they should be propelled forthwith into our 'proper programme' is some measure of the cultural arrogance and ignorance of those supposedly adept at responding to individual needs.

We decided instead to organise 'Second Chance' — a one-day-a-week, serious and committed programme for women, in which we could build upon what we had learned at neighbourhood level, and which could begin to provide the kinds of resources and opportunities which would take seriously the social, economic and political conditions of women, as well as their rights to decent educational provision.

'Second Chance for Women'

Recruitment

In the summer of 1979 we began publicising 'Second Chance for Women', and at this point our aims were quite simple. We were concerned to redistribute the kind of educational opportunities which well-satisfied adult students in the most favourable kind of learning environments are entitled to expect, to those who, for a variety of social, political and economic reasons, had received least from the education system in the past. This meant positive discrimination in favour of women and working-class women in particular. It was to be 'serious education', not the kind of 'low-profile' variety which gets smuggled by stealth into community centres, mothers-and-toddlers groups and gatherings of women on housing estates — slipping in between the afternoon 'cuppa' and the organisation of the jumble sale — fearful of being seen to be serious, and as a result failing to take seriously the educational needs of the women involved.

The question of 'relevance' was critical from the beginning. As we have seen earlier, patriarchal ideas about 'social relevance' in adult education are highly dependent upon professional perceptions about women's domestic homemaking and child-bearing roles. We began with the assumption that the traditional roles of women are discriminatory and restricting ones, so that rather than offering curriculum content designed to reaffirm or reinforce them, we adopted a different definition of social relevance as our starting point. The topics chosen for study were to provide a vehicle for the examination of the shared condition of being female in our society, to examine how sexism and patriarchy operates, what the consequences of this might be for ordinary women and what, if anything, can be done to escape from the limited and limiting expectations which a society like ours still reserves for women. Clearly we were offering an initiation into feminism.

We were also offering an introduction to the study of law, literature, sociology, politics and history, though in a form which is uncommon in university adult education. We have seen how Women's Studies are by nature inter-disciplinary, and how they consequently 'subvert the traditional boundaries between subjects'.[8] As we were soon to discover in practice, because of the ways in which such knowledge has been produced in the past, and given the ways in which it is still most frequently disseminated, our approach soon began to question both its traditional authority and purpose.

The intention of the publicity was to produce a message which was unintimidating and encouraging, which left no one in any doubt about the educational opportunities available and the need for serious commitment, but which guaranteed flexibility and plenty of help to those selected. We made it clear that we did not expect any formal qualifications, that it did not matter if women felt 'rusty' so far as studying was concerned, and in making the course cheap with easily waivable fees, in providing resource packs of reading materials and in providing a crèche, we tried to remove, so far as we were able, the financial exclusivity of university adult education. Most important, perhaps, we advertised the course explicitly for working-class women.

The response was really quite astonishing, given the confidential wisdoms which many adult educators use to explain the 'non-participation' of working-class adults in education — lack of confidence, lack of commitment and lack of interest. Over 120 women enquired about the course, and more than three times as many women as we had places for actually applied.[9] This pattern has been repeated in subsequent years as the course has become locally better known and enthusiastic students have passed on information about it to their neighbours and friends. This kind of response from 'professional feminists' or 'inveterate course-goers' would probably be considered unexceptional — though none of the more traditional courses in our extramural programme seem to attract this amount of attention. How is it to be explained?

Looking back at the application forms again, we find that few of the women who apply each year identify their expectations in the socialist and feminist terms which we use among ourselves to justify our enthusiasms. One of them said, 'I consider myself a feminist but I don't know how to practise it in my life, or how to help organise myself or other women to create more possibilities for women'. Another said, 'the idea of learning with women about other women is possibly the only way of getting over past difficulties'. The majority talked in terms of their own lack of confidence or lack of purpose.

There are lots of things I would love to do but as I am no longer sure I am capable of doing them I tend to hesitate and end up not even trying.

Since I have stopped working I have become less confident.

I have had a number of jobs, some like Sales Rep/Merchandiser with an HGV licence — were those in which men would normally be employed. But in these situations I have always felt inadequate or insecure . . . I felt I lacked the intellectual knowledge I seemed to need.

I need more out of life than being a housekeeper and being at the beck and call of my family. Also I feel that I have become a vegetable since giving up work.

I do not think I can continue my present life-style without going scatty.

I want to equip myself to do something which will absorb me when the children no longer need me. I don't want to be lumbered with some soul-destroying factory work.

I'm not very good at putting what I feel on paper. I hope you understand the desperation that is behind these words.
Please don't refuse me because I'm 50. I feel that I have another ten years of working life but I don't want to spend it washing other peoples dishes. I'm so tired of being told I'm old and unskilled. My family has grown up and no longer depends on me so much . . . now I don't really know what I can do or what I'm capable of. I'm inclined to be self-conscious and feel embarassed easily — I do hope this makes sense to you. I would like to do something worthwhile and feel I can still achieve something in my life.

One woman certainly knew what was wrong — not only for her, but for many women like her — but didn't know what to do about it. She hoped the course would be able to help.

I think I will find the topics that will be discussed very interesting. The main attraction of this course for me is that it is for working-class women like myself. I have always been a great supporter of women's rights, this comes about mainly because of my personal experiences. Last year I had the misfortune to have to spend a night at a battered wives' home. I talked to the other women a lot and was appalled by their experiences, the home was very overcrowded and the conditions bad. I was 'laughed at' by policemen when I went to the station to report my husband for rape, in spite of the fact that I had slept in a different room from him for some months and divorce proceedings were well underway. My bruises didn't make any impression either. I have been the subject of many unpleasant remarks because I have to rely on social security and because I am a woman alone I constantly find people trying to take advantage of me, and married friends are afraid I will seduce their husbands because they imagine I am frustrated. I think this course will be helpful to me if I am fortunate enough to get selected.

Although the application form is very simple and deliberately unthreatening, one woman — who subsequently turned out to have been a national schools' diving champion, to have taken herself off to the United States at 17 to work as a nanny, to have been a swimming instructor on the Queen Mary, and to have done all kinds of different jobs from factory and shop work to psychiatric nursing, photo-printing and proof-reading — after a lengthy period of child-rearing and housework was sufficiently undermined by that experience to write in answer to the question, 'Please give details of any job or other personal experience you think is relevant to your application for this course'; 'I would like to attend this course in the hope that I might gain some confidence and assessment of my own potential — especially to answer questions like this without feeling totally useless'. Most of the women who apply are very open about their personal circumstances, their divorces, their children, their frustrations and loneliness, but not surprisingly, perhaps, most of them describe personal problems with varying degrees of self-blame and failure.

Of course all this would be 'meat and drink' to those imbued with 'the sense of mission' endemic in so much of the work associated with outreach and community education. Adult Basic Education has a whole language of personal deficit and disadvantage and countless assumptions about the fecklessness and failings of individuals who are 'unable to cope' with life as they live it.[10] All kinds of remedial curricula and confidence-inducing treatment, designed to develop 'coping skills' and to provide 'role education' rapidly spring to mind. No doubt readers will be familiar with the local variations of the kinds of education provision I am referring to.[11] Nell Keddie dismisses them almost without exception as 'bad faith' and as a way in which the 'concept of individual need and student-centredness' based on a pathological model of the individual is used

> to legitimate an ideological commitment by adult education to the *status quo* in which the educator's perception of needs . . . derives from a concept of disadvantage which seeks to remedy social problems through the imputed inadequacies of individuals.[12]

Needless to say, this is not the way in which we interpret what we find written on the application forms. Women from an early age are socialised into accepting a position in the social relations of production which isolates and excludes them from much direct participation in the class struggle or in any other form of political action. They derive their status secondhand from their fathers and their husbands, and once they take on their traditional domestic role in the sexual division of labour, and make their traditional contribution to the reproduction of children within the nuclear family, they become isolated in a very real way from each other.

Although many may be dissatisfied with their domestic isolation and the constraints which keep large numbers of them as unpaid houseworkers and underpaid workers, the careful fostering of 'feminine qualities' in women has effectively helped to discourage them from seeking or attaining power and status in their own right. Since men and women are conventionally defined in relation to each other, and because women occupy relatively disadvantaged positions in relation to male wage-earners, they come in time to undervalue themselves. It is not surprising that this often becomes expressed as 'lack of confidence' and for many women takes the form of serious and profound depression. As Hilary Wainwright points out,

> Much of the oppression of women takes place 'in private', in areas of life considered 'personal'. The causes of that oppression are social and economic, but these causes can only be revealed and confronted when women challenge the assumptions of their personal life, of who does the housework, of the way children are brought up, the quality of friendships, even the way we make love and with whom.[13]

These are not normally the subjects of discussion among women, let alone part of the curriculum of education or the basis of political action except in the women's movement.

It is not surprising, therefore, that women express their dissatisfactions in ways which are not immediately intended as such, but which can later be codified as feminist issues: the sense of failure received from schooling, the prospect of looking for work with no qualifications, the feeling of lost or displaced identity and lack of confidence, a sense of injustice about the hardships endured by women, and, in almost every case, remarks that demonstrate dissatisfaction with a life limited by domestic reponsibilities and traditional, low-paid women's work.

Each year, as course organiser, I spend three weeks during the summer talking individually to almost all of the women who are being considered for the course. I am aware that the notion of 'formal selection' goes very much against the grain in adult education, although the extent to which the cultural character of mainstream provision effectively screens the active participation of working-class and black students can be seen as a system of covert selection. But quite simply we do not have the resources to give places to all of those who apply. The purpose of the interview is to ensure that positive discrimination in favour of working-class women who are keen to learn, and who are anxious to make some use of the learning, is achieved. It would be very easy to fill the course three times over with women who have already experienced a fair amount of education and who are relatively privileged. The extent to which middle-class women identify with the aims of the course and also experience social isolation and role frustration despite their more comfortable circumstances worries me as a feminist. To exclude anyone because of the middle-class status they have derived from their husbands seems wrong, and hopefully as we secure more resources this will be no longer necessary.

In 1979 we recruited 33 students, 13 more than we had originally planned for. They were, with some exceptions, working-class women. 19 out of the 33 had no formal qualifications — the rest, an odd O-level; or CSE. Twenty-two out of the 33 had no previous experience of adult education classes, 12 out of the 33 were single parents, the majority of those who worked were employed part-time in unskilled and low-paid jobs, and at least a third were dependent on state benefits.

In 1980 we offered places to 41 women. Their average age was just over 30, although they ranged from 24 to 51. All of them had children and some had part-time jobs — mostly domestic, catering and shop work. Half were single parents dependent on state benefits, and the majority had no formal qualifications. Each year the student profile has been similar; we have not in principle given places to women with higher education or to women who are using Second Chance as a way of changing professions.

We divide the students into two groups — one group meeting on a Tuesday and one group meeting on a Thursday. A crèche is provided, and the very nominal fees are waived in every circumstance which would prevent a woman from taking part.

Curriculum Matters

Tessa Blackstone argues that whilst higher pay is perhaps the most important way of improving the confidence of women and their image of themselves,

another is through education. Better-educated women are more likely to be politically active, to be employed, to believe in sex equality and to be less likely to avoid situations of conflict'.[14]

According to Rosemary Deem, women have a choice about such things,

> to stay as they are, or to try to alter their position so that they have greater equality with men. The first choice they possess as individuals, the second they will only achieve collectively. The responsibility of women in education is not only to educate and persuade other women to fight for changes, whether these are legislative, organisational or attitudinal, but also to educate and persuade men that changes are necessary, not just in education but in the whole organisation of society.[15]

We made the decision to begin with women, but the wider issues have rapidly become apparent. The content of Second Chance is principally about women and is taught exclusively by women. The courage, self-esteem and solidarity which the women's movement, freed from male interference, has given to so many women, also creates in Second Chance a learning environment which encourages women to define their own needs, express their own personalities and discover their own identities unconstrained by the super-ordinate—subordinate character of male—female relationships. Women learning together with other women can resist the compulsion to become part of the dehumanising forces of competition, elitism and self-aggrandisement encouraged by patriarchal systems of education, and choose instead to reflect the different kinds of power and strength that exist — for instance, women's strong capacity to care for others — a quality often buried, diffused, misdirected or incorporated under patriarchy, but which redefined, contains the energy to in turn redefine human relationships. In formulating the curriculum for Second Chance we have been conscious of four important considerations: that we should reflect as much as possible the circumstances and realities of the women on the course; that essentially female and class cultural experience should be validated; that we should encourage the exploration of information and knowledge likely to heighten the feminist consciousness of students; and that we should not underestimate the intelligence of our students to wrestle with complex ideas.

Our expectations of the students are enormous — not for competitive or elitist reasons, but because to be anything less is patronising and restrictive. We have found that a combination of specifically challenging and totally encouraging support enables each to revalue her own ability and to contemplate doing more than she imagines herself capable of achieving. Seen in this light the rewards are many and various — to enjoy a book which previously would have seemed intimidating, to complete a piece of writing that sets down argument and discussion in a satisfying way, to discuss and debate issues which at one time seemed the prerogative of others, and to work collectively on a project in which co-operation and complementary strengths rather than competition are the secret of its satisfaction — all these enable us to reconstitute learning as a pleasurable and confirming experience.

Of course it might be possible to encourage this kind of interested enthusiasm and positive fulfilment using 'any old knowledge' — but I doubt it. The combination of exploring and creating knowlege about women, with women, for women, and in a way which values women, and makes bridges between us is, I think, dangerous and revolutionary business so far as patriarchy is concerned, but liberationary so far as women are concerned.

The Morning Sessions

The morning sessions are given over to an examination from the point of view of women of themes like family life, employment and the economy, the politics of welfare, the struggle for the vote, women under attack and the inequalities commensurate with class, race and gender oppression. A resource pack of reading materials is provided for each topic and a seminar–discussion approach is usual. Because so-called 'academic knowledge' traditionally relies upon strong authority and strict subject boundaries, it can become regarded as a form of 'private property' with its own power structure and market value. As Bernstein points out, any disturbances in the classification of knowledge can lead to disturbances in existing authority structures, specific educational identities and concepts of property.[16] Inter-disciplinary approaches can threaten the authority of those who have a vested career interest in preserving subject boundaries. And team teaching in which tutors contribute not usually as subject specialists but in relation to each other can be quite challenging to those who have long hidden behind the authority of their specialisms, or conducted their business 'in private' with students 'at their feet'.

Happily these concerns do not trouble us too much ideologically, although it has taken us some time to develop genuine inter-disciplinary and team-teaching approaches which also recognise and include the existing knowledge and experience of the students. And I think we still have a long way to go before we can claim to have consistently matched practice with philosophy in this respect. The debate with others in our professional reference groups is not so much one of consistency between philosophy and practice, however, but more about the value of the philosophy and the approaches which it encourages. For those who make a career out of 'being an expert' and holding fairly elitist ideas about quality and excellence, it has been usual to dismiss our work as eclectic or superficial. But since the criteria of excellence in practice often relies upon essentially didactic teaching methods, students' inactivity and a preoccupation with 'keeping up the numbers to keep the class alive', it seems hardly worth arguing about — except in so far as the relegation of our work to the margins of mainstream university adult education makes it vulnerable.

What is more important than fruitless debates about 'quality and excellence' is the extent to which an inter-disciplinary approach to knowledge questions the traditional authority and purpose of that knowledge. These issues become clear in the discussions about legal matters and 'women and health', for example, in which it rapidly becomes apparent that prevailing definitions about what constitutes 'female behaviour' in these areas are deeply rooted in patriarchal assumptions and controls over the creation, selection and dissemination of legal and medical knowledge.

The inclusion of Sociology and Law in Second Chance has relied profoundly on the experience of women in the group — many of them the victims of insensitive and outrageous legal assumptions about women. This piece of writing by a student in our first course led to an examination of the laws relating to domestic violence, the attitude of judges, the police, social workers and housing officials. We were also able to probe some of the less wholesome aspects of heterosexual love which make all women the potential victims of male violence.

I had gone to bed to try to get rid of a headache. The front door opened with a bang, I lay there pretending to be asleep. He stamped up the stairs into the bedroom and over to the bed. I felt the bedcovers being pulled and then I was on the floor. I stood up and faced him. I didn't smile (it might irritate him). I didn't look straight at him (it might irritate him). I didn't cry (it might irritate him). I just stood there. He started shouting at me asking why I was in bed early. I tried to explain about my headache. He wouldn't listen — he wanted something to eat. So I turned to go out of the bedroom and downstairs to the kitchen. He grabbed me at the top of the stairs yelling that I wasn't to walk away when he was talking to me. I tried to go downstairs. He pushed me. The stairs had two bends, I hit my head on the wall and rolled half way down. Before I could stand up he kicked me. I went the rest of the way down to the bottom. Now I stood up. It was a mistake. He punched me on the side of the head. I fell down and he kicked me. This time I stayed down. He walked into the kitchen and filled the kettle, lit the gas and put the kettle on the cooker. Slowly I stood up and walked towards the bathroom. Then I felt him behind me. In panic I opened the front door and ran out of the house. I ran down the road to the corner, then I had to stop because I couldn't breathe. Leaning on the fence I looked at myself. My nose was bleeding, my head was ringing and I was sure that I wasn't able to hear properly. But above all was the pain in my chest. Every time I drew breath I had a stabbing pain. I remember thinking 'oh Christ he's cracked a rib'. I realised that I was only wearing a cotton nightdress. I had nothing on my feet. I leaned against the fence trying to make sense of what had just happened, vowing not to go back into the house because now he was going to be very angry. At least the kids had been asleep. The kids! Oh God, I had forgotten the kids. I had to go back, there was no telling what he would do to them if I didn't. He had never hit them before but I lived in terror that he might one day. There was nowhere to go. My parents were long dead. There were no refuges I could go to and my neighbours didn't want to know. So, fully aware that when I got back into the house, he was going to start hitting me again and again, I turned and walked back into the house. Hating myself for being such a coward, for not being able to make my marriage work. For in some way being responsible for the beating I was about to receive. 'Oh God don't let him hit me where it shows, my face is going to take some explaining already'. He was standing at the front door waiting for me. I walked towards him. I didn't cry (it might irritate him). I didn't smile (it might irritate him) I didn't look straight at him (it might irritate him) I walked under his arm and into the house. The next day I tried to commit suicide with a razor blade. I failed at that as well.

Sue Atkins, one of the course tutors on Second Chance, comments,

> The teaching of law and the knowledge and skills to really understand the law can enable women to utilise that understanding in ways they choose. In relation to women the teaching of law may serve a more primary aim of encouraging among women the perception of themselves as an interest group sharing common social and economic conditions and with special interests to defend in society. It may be that for some women such an understanding will encourage the kind of impetus which is necessary to enable them, in co-operation with others, to begin challenging the latent assumptions and restrictions imposed upon them both by the law and by other patriarchal systems.[17]

When we considered the National Health Service the personal accounts of depression, childbirth experiences, and unwanted pregnancies, together with the testimonies of those who had worked as nurses, hospital cleaners and ancillary workers in a male-dominated and rapidly disintegrating service, all provided authentic knowledge about women's lives which we could not have found in the male academic tradition or within the encoded knowledge of our subject specialisms, and yet they have all been shared and been the basis of our development.

> 'Are you always so slow?' More of a statement than a question and coming from one of the many white coats at the end of the bed. I'd always vowed I'd never have a baby in hospital — so what was I doing here in ward A2 of St Mary's hospital for my fifth confinement? The bait was sterilisation to be carried out following the birth. I'd given birth to four babies in the comfort of my own home, in my own way, in my own time. Family around me, a cup of tea here, peeling the spuds there — a quick drag of a cigarette when I liked. Getting into bed literally the last moment to produce the child. The friendliness of the pupil midwife — now a friend after nine months of regular visits — the atmosphere of reproduction as it should be — joyful and relaxed. This time, not to be. The constant examinations. Was I

sure of my dates? 'Funny the head isn't engaged. Have a feel and see what you think'. And the umpteenth internal examination on admission (because I was overdue!) I automatically flinched when I saw a pair of rubber gloves. Strapped to a 'drip' to get me going, pillows all along my back to stop me turning over and the bell out of reach, it was obvious that I was out of favour. Staff had planned the birth for teatime, now it was clear I was going to cause the night staff some work. The doctor decided to break my water. After poking around for what seemed an age, whilst I fixed my gaze and my thoughts on an abstract something far away — he waved the forceps in front of me, exclaiming triumphantly, 'Now you know what colour hair your baby has'. In the forceps was a bloodstained clump of hair. What the hell did he think he was doing! I no longer felt proud to be giving birth — I felt dirty — a specimen on a slab. I finally gave birth to my son seventeen hours later — healthy — but with an inch-long scab along his scalp.[18]

I had tried hot baths, hot gin and nutmeg, punching myself in the stomach, large black pills from a bent chemist and hot glycerine on a tampon. After sixteen weeks I was still pregnant . . . Soon after we went to a large private house in an expensive part of Southsea to see the gynaecologist. He was a portly middle-aged Scot in a flashy suit, his fat fingers adorned with large gold rings. He asked how I'd become pregnant I tried to explain. He interrupted saying that he'd seen far too many pregnancies blamed on a bottle of gin and that in his opinion I must sub-consciously want a child. 'Look' I wanted to say 'I'm a Lesbian; there's no room in my life for bloody kids', but my mother was there and that stopped me. Up on the couch, after the internal (Mother looked on) he said, 'Presumably you do have sexually excitable feelings? . . . Meanwhile the gynaecologist asked my mother, 'Don't you remember what it was like to be young?' 'Yes' she said 'I was no angel'. 'Well then, don't expect her to be'. 'I didn't even know she had a boyfriend'. 'How old is she, twenty?' 'Of course she has a boyfriend. All girls her age do'. He took me into another room to write the cheque. There he said, 'You want this child don't you?' 'No' I said 'It's like a cancer'. Away from my mother I was too guilt-ridden to tell him the one thing I thought might alter his opinion. Back in the other room, he told my mother he wouldn't end my pregnancy and stood his ground in the face of her tearful entreaties. Out in the cold night she rounded on me. 'That was a waste of money wasn't it?' 'My money' I said (over a week's wages actually) 'You told him you wanted it didn't you?' Ironic to consider, eleven years on, that another professional man might soon decide that my proud, splendid daughter shouldn't live with her mother as lesbians shouldn't bring up children, should they?[19]

Dr Norm is a consultant in a busy general hospital and Monday is the day he does his round on ward 4 . . . The phone is ringing, two porters are demanding that nurses lift patients from beds to stretchers because their union has told them they don't have to do it in case they hurt their backs. A patient's relatives are demanding information, and two junior nurses have just dropped Mrs Batty out of the hoist into a bath from a height of ten feet, resulting in screams that can be heard a mile away, or more to the point, by the now anxious relatives. However amidst the daily chaos of ward life Dr Norm has appeared with his retinue of registrars, housemen and medical students — rather like Jesus Christ with a band of awestruck disciples waiting for his pearls of wisdom and longing to touch the hem of his white coat. The signs of impatience begin to show on his face. 'I am ready sister, shall we proceed?' he says and marches through the surrounding chaos to the first bed. During his round Sister and her Staff Nurse will be constantly at his beck and call. They are trained to know exactly what he will want next and will be there at the ready with the necessary equipment for the next examination. They will also clear up after him as he goes, to the extent that when he peels off his dirty rubber gloves and drops them behind him without turning, a receiver will be there to catch them. From the patients Dr Norm will receive endless gratitude and deference as he moves from bed to bed like a benevolent God blessing the sick and needy — reassuring, always charming, seldom truthful. Who are they to be told the truth about what ails them? They wouldn't understand anyway. Now and then a small voice of discontent may be heard, but this is quickly silenced with a few well chosen words of caution which soon make the patient who dares to question realise that she is the last person who should know anything of the workings or not workings of her own body.

Only when Dr Norm enters the small side-room, in which sits

his private patient, does his attitude change. The man is paying for his treatment, not through National Insurance like the others, but paying Dr Norm personally and very handsomely with cheques and bottles of gin and whisky. And for this reason Dr Norm is prepared to take one or two steps down from his pedestal and talk man to man with his patient. Not equal to equal however. That would never do. After all the man is sick and frightened. Frightened enough to pay dearly to jump the queue and as such Dr Norm knows that he is in a very superior position. After all this man needs him. He tells his private patients the same old lies in a far more expensive tone of voice. It is 11.30 am now and the round is finished. The master and his entourage disappear into Sister's office and she busies herself making them coffee and serving them biscuits whilst they discuss the patients. She has trained for four years and had ten years' experience in her speciality, but when they leave she washes up after them and puts the china neatly away for another day.[20]

These are angry statements, from women usually encouraged to keep quiet; but creative anger, focused with the precision that has the power to clarify and liberate us from our delusions, in preparation for progress and change. Barbara Hancock, another course tutor, reaffirms our commitment to releasing this anger and taking its implications seriously.

I think the key reason for the impact of the course is the women themselves and who they are. The nature of the course is determined by them. What Second Chance has done is to bring together a group of women who are committed to learning. What they learn they learn mainly from each other through the experience, the personality and the ideas each woman brings with her.
The role of the course is to provide a framework and an atmosphere in which this sharing can take place and to provide some additional ideas and ways of thinking that can help women to review their own life experience and that of those around them.[21]

Discussions about the politics of welfare and government responses to poverty have focused on the differences between pathological and structural explanations of inequality. These themes have produced some of our most heated and politicising debates. Anne Farwell's personal outrage at the injustice of poverty and her anguish brought about by capitalist materialism and inhumanity, because of the respect she was accorded by all those who shared that year with her, exercised considerable influence on the thinking of other women in the group. But she also had the capacity to use satire as a telling weapon.

Daily Reader 25th June
There is still no information as to the whereabouts of Sir Keith Joseph. Sir Keith was abducted from his London home ten weeks ago. A militant feminist group, I.M. F.E.D. U.P. (International Movement for the Elimination of Drudgery and Unpaid Prostitution) have claimed responsibility for the abduction and have said that Sir Keith is undergoing corrective therapy.
Sir Keith was abducted after his speech advocating the sterilisation of working-class women, and expounding his theories of a master race.

Daily Reader 26th June
The abductors of Sir Keith Joseph, I.M. F.E.D. U.P., issued the following statement today:
'We released Sir Keith this morning. He is now tame and completely domesticated. During his stay with us, Sir Keith has been incarcerated with no companionship, and subjected to continuous video-taped television commercials and uninterrupted washing up. When we released him, he rushed off to Tesco to buy some "white wonder" detergent, and a tin of "Whizzo" lavatory cleaner. He was last seen applying for a job as a charlady in Peckham Underground station'.

Daily Reader 27th June
Sir Keith Joseph arrived home today after his ten-week abduction. Sir Keith's personal physician, Sir Harley Street, said that Sir Keith was suffering from cerebral atrophy and galloping consumeritis. Sir Harley said there was no hope of Sir Keith's recovery. Sir Keith himself said that he was retiring from public life in order to devote more time to his housework.[22]

One of last year's students perhaps sums up best the usual atmosphere of Second Chance learning as 'the warmth, the camaraderie, the discussions in a deadly serious world — even though the subject matter has been deadly serious, the way we learn and participate has been fun'. Others insist, 'I can honestly say, I don't think I've ever enjoyed a year of my life so much'.

The Afternoon Sessions

The Afternoon sessions are intended to complement the essentially 'information and analysis-based' approach in the morning sessions, in which the topics of study, though flexible, are generally planned by the tutors. In the afternoons we use a workshop approach in which the content is entirely determined by the students.

During the year all women take part in a writer's workshop, and choose between a variety of other options which in 1980–1, for example, included an oral herstory group, a radio workshop, a film group and a special projects group. The aims of the writers' workshops are not to encourage 'creative writing' as such, or to indulge in 'literary criticism' or to perfect 'grammar and communication skills'. The main concern is to explore the condition of being a woman in our society through discussion and personal writing about first-hand experience. The experiences which women choose to write about become the experiences discussed and shared within the groups and have included among many others childhood memories, working lives, relationships with men, low income, family life, depression and repression. They also provide the setting in which personal experience can be shared with others, and in which the links between personal experience and shared conditions can be measured — a process which the women's movement in other circumstances might refer to as 'consciousness raising'. In our groups it certainly enables women to voice their own feelings about feminity, sexism, childbirth and domestic violence, for example, whilst listening to, and learning from, the experience of others. The confidence of writing for and discussing with other women in a totally non-competitive way encourages a good deal of frank discussion about the illusions which many women are expected to subscribe to. A lot of time is spent with social and political questions, whilst at other times explicit and satirical condemnation of men's attitudes and behaviour towards women enables us all to laugh at or be angry about and put into some kind of general perspective the day-to-day difficulties of living in a society which subordinates women. It would be too much to claim that the support and intimacy between women in these groups enables them 'at a stroke' to begin to revalue themselves as women and to begin to take stands against subordination in their own lives. Such unity of insight and action is riven through with contradictions among even the most ardent of 'practising feminists'. But certainly for many, the recognition that other women 'feel the same' and are struggling to escape from assorted identities which they do not particularly like is a great mutual strength. Interestingly, the language used to express all of this bears very little resemblance to the language of Women's Liberation and its current jargon, though the underlying sentiments are the same.

Julia Kellaway, writing specifically about the writers' workshops, comments on characteristics that are equally true of the other workshops.

> One thing that emerged was just how much energy and hope we were all investing in the Second Chance course, which for many people had been interpreted individually to mean last chance . . . Disappointment was always a possibility, and that some people would get bruised by the experience of the workshops, either because they discovered too much about themselves and were dissatisfied, or because they discovered too much about the rest of society for comfort, also seemed to be inevitable. But the strength of the workshop for most people lay in the discovery that they were not alone. Individually people discovered that other people shared their thoughts and feelings about women in society and about men; politically this gave people a base for conceiving of action, whether through writing, demanding rights, demanding a voice or actually organising. People who had been confined to the house and family, or to living on the poverty line, or both, discovered that there was a possibility of acting collectively with other people.[23]

On a few occasions now we have published some of our writing and distributed our radio tapes,[24] not out of any commercial or pretentious motivation, but because we wanted to share what we have produced with others. And in addition, whether through the publication of personal writing, the production of radio programmes, a video film or the collection of first-hand accounts of women's lives, the workshops have also enabled us to contribute to expanding women's culture as a radical alternative to bourgeois and patriarchal definitions of 'proper' cultural expression — a process which adds to the store of recorded wisdom from which other women both inside and outside the women's movement can learn.

The Purpose of Knowledge

Most challenging of all, perhaps, are questions about the purpose of knowledge — both in terms of how established definitions of knowledge have been used to maintain cultural domination and control in class and sexual terms, and also what the purpose of acquiring knowledge might be so far as students are concerned.

For the majority of middle-class students in mainstream education 'the purpose of knowledge' rarely presents a problem. For undergraduates it is frequently something which they have to acquire to pass their examinations. Once the examination is passed, the knowledge can be forgotten along with the rest of the things they learned and subsequently forgot at O and A-level. Enlightened educators might argue that amassing knowledge is less important than developing skills of logic, discovery and analysis. But whichever variation is preferred the purpose, in vocational terms, is instrumental. For students in traditional adult education classes knowledge may also be instrumental in the sense of confirming images they have of themselves as consumers of culture, or if they are women, as those responsible for managing and servicing the home. But so far as 'the great tradition' is concerned, knowledge 'for its own sake' is thought to be sufficient. Lawson makes much of 'the essence' of adult education and of its 'traditional role of general cultural diffusion and personal development through studies on a broad perspective'.[25] He is very critical of education which can be described as narrowly instrumental — by which he means the pre-occupation in a good deal of community education with welfare rights, trade union studies and para-political action. Of course for working-class students knowledge and education have to be instrumental. That is not to say that they might not come to enjoy educational activities 'for their own sake', but to make any real sense, education has to be a tool. It might be a way of getting more money or putting yourself in a position to have more choice and better prospects in the job market as this comment illustrates,

no matter what happens I certainly want to continue with my education, but I really want to do something which will help me career-wise. I have never worked 'on the cards'. Some may think that's great but it's not. You can't imagine the hassle or the barely hidden doubts about my ability or enthusiasm for work when I say I have no NI number, can furnish no particulars or references from past employment. You never get out of the rut because no one will give you a chance.

Looked at in class or feminist terms, however, the purpose of knowledge has to be more than a purely individualistic solution to personal disadvantage. Social change, liberation, if you like in a general sense, will be achieved only by collective as distinct from individual responses to oppression. If the links between personal experience and shared conditions are well made, the purpose of education takes on an added significance. Some understanding of the ways in which class and patriarchal society operates to subordinate some groups, to diminish their status and to restrict their control over the conditions which most significantly affect their lives, is the first line of defence against these restrictions. To be able to re-examine personal problems in the social context of sexual inequality and the shared condition of being female in a society like ours, opens up the possibility of collective as distinct from purely personal responses. To discover that working-class disadvantage is rooted not in failure or inferiority, but in the economic and cultural dominance exercised by those who have historically been able to control and influence economic, social and political institutions, suggests the need for collective as distinct from individual resistance. One student puts it like this,

The real me has emerged during this course, and after years of frustration and anger, discovering my own sense of identity and being able to take a critical look at myself and my life has given me tremendous confidence. I have always spoken out over things in society that I feel are wrong or unjust, but its always been in isolation and I never felt confident enough to be absolutely sure of my motives.

I was rebellious at school, my parents said they had never been able to control me as a child and when I joined a trade union in 1958 I was called a trouble maker — so I actually came to believe that I had some kind of uncontrollable illness. It never occurred to me until the Second Chance course (and as a direct result of what I have learned on that course) that I had a right to feel proud of my actions . . . Because of my new found confidence along with the feeling of solidarity among the other women on the course any conflicts other people feel about me I increasingly see as their problem and not mine. Providing I don't set out deliberately to hurt anyone I will defend the right to be 'me' without any restrictions — I won't compromise anymore as I've done for most of my life. The discovery of feminism has set all the bells ringing, has begun to give me some of the answers I was looking for and liberated me from my guilt. I have been able to see my problems as political and not personal.

Meeting other women who feel the same has resulted in a great feeling of sisterhood and friendship. I begin to see women in their own right — not just as wives and mothers. I feel like I've discovered women for the first time and also how much I care about them. I don't want to go onto college or university or anything like that in case it takes me away again. I want to work with women because together we have a lot of work to do.

In adult education the struggle for social relevance and a curriculum related to social change is, as we have seen, not new.[26] It characterised the popular political movements of the nineteenth century, and was the distinguishing feature of women's education in the Co-operative Guilds and the early trade union movement. Almost a century later the same concern to ensure that education provides 'really useful knowledge' which can be linked to social and political action and which gives women the confidence to stand up for themselves, is an important ingredient of Second Chance.

This doesn't mean that some of our students are not interested in moving into some other form of further or higher education or exerting the right to train for jobs usually considered masculine. The challenge made to male and middle-class monopolies in this respect is an important way of increasing women's power in society. But the conviction with which many of them discuss learning as a collective enterprise rather than an act of individual self-improvement, and as a way of gathering knowledge and developing skills which can't be 'taken back into' work with other women particularly, is a version of the 'useful knowledge debate' which is conspicuously absent from most professional discussions about continuing education.

Student Reactions

Making generalisations about students' reactions is difficult because I suspect that they have valued the course in different ways to different degrees and for different reasons. But there are one or two observations which seem worth commenting on here.

The first is the high level of commitment and motivation which most students share. Given that no one *has* to come and no one *has* to speak a sentence or write a word if she doesn't want to — being able to count on women's willingness to become deeply involved in the many different activities and issues which emerge proves to be the least of our problems. And this does not just mean discussion, reading books and writing essays — although there is plenty of all these — it has meant for some, attending women's rights conferences and other political meetings, it has meant taking part in the TUC's Day of Action against the cuts in public spending, writing a joint submission to the Law Commission about proposed changes in the illegitimacy laws, collecting local evidence about education cuts and writing countless letters to the press, MPs and local councillors about the effects of reducing spending. It has meant producing publications and radio programmes and developing a women's history archive. It has meant fund-raising, women's theatre trips, and giving talks about the course to other groups. It has meant for some a visit to a women's group in Le Havre, and for 55 women in the summer of 1981 a residential weekend which for many represented the only time they have been away from home on their own since their last confinement. Some individuals have become increasingly involved in neighbourhood action groups, local advice centres, their trade unions and political parties. In 1982 the same woman who said 'please don't refuse me because I'm 50 — I'm so tired of being told I'm old and unskilled' stood as a candidate in the local elections. The majority have remained involved in some form of related educational activities after each course has finished, and several have gone on to further and full-time higher education.

Given the variety and enthusiasm of all these developments, the narrow and limited expectations which adult education at all levels so frequently reserves for women seems to have been well challenged. And it is interesting to note the change in emphasis expressed by our students at the end of the course, as a consequence of having done all these things, compared with the reasons they gave for applying in the first place. You will remember how many of them explained weaknesses in a personal way, but how we consciously rejected the usual adult education prescriptions intended to 'treat' women 'lacking education' and 'lacking confidence' with none-too-palatable doses of 'basic education', 'coping skills', 'group therapy' and 'role education'. Presumably 'the cure' measured in these terms would depend upon how much more confident women became in performing basic skills, and coping with or adapting to their roles of wives and mothers.

Women on our course certainly speak about feeling more confident at the end of the year, not because their conventional roles are confirmed, but rather because a resistance to their limitations is encouraged.

Since I started on the Second Chance for Women course I have become a person rather than being a mother and housewife.

The self-discipline at first was difficult, adjusting to making time *for myself*, sometimes I questioned what the hell I was doing, but I'm glad I persevered because now I feel motivated to expand even more, which has given me greater confidence in myself above the usual housewife role.

I now have direction instead of feeling as if I were drowning. It helps a lot when you realise it's not only you who feels suffocated without understanding why: there are too many women who feel the same.

I feel now as if I've rediscovered myself as a person after years of being office dogsbody, girlfriend, wife or mother. After 3 years of being at home, a typical bored housewife, I feel that my horizons have opened out beyond my wildest hopes — I feel capable of almost anything — as if my life has been given back to me.

I may appear enthusiastic about the course but honestly, I don't know what I'd have done without it — it's made me open my mouth as well as my eyes.

I feel more confident about my place in society as a woman. I have learned a lot that has helped me put my point of view across much more effectively. Knowledge is power as they say.

I now care about issues which I didn't believe had anything to do with me.

I am getting more politically aware now and I will query and question people who make decisions on my behalf whereas before I would have shrugged my shoulders helplessly and walked away. But now I won't.

I'm no different to many other women with a home and family to care for. But there's part of 'me' that wants to be seen as 'me' 'myself' 'in my own right'.

This course has helped a lot. It's made me a different person and I feel it's brought qualities out of me I always felt I had but never been able to show or use because of lack of education. The course has given me a whole new purpose in life and a whole new outlook on things. It's as if I've been given an ever open book. I'm learning from it all the time but finding something new and exciting still left to discover.

I see my future now as 'participating' in life and not like a spectator as I was before.

The feeling of acquiring *new* knowledge obviously plays a big part in all of this. The general reaction after topics in which we discussed, for example, legal changes affecting illegitimacy, the impact of public spending cuts, the weaknesses of the equal opportunities legislation, the treatment of women criminals, the hidden subsidies which support private medicine and private education, etc., was 'if only more people knew about these things'. This was knowledge which raised consciousness about social and political issues, not knowledge to be saved up and stored out of context of real-life struggles. For some it challenged a cosy complacency, for others it provided the ammunition they needed to support opinions they had always felt but sometimes had difficulty in defending. In traditional forms of education the acquisition of knowledge and the intellectual skills defined to manage it are usually given precedence over considerations about the ways in which knowledge originates and is used. So far as our students are concerned knowledge 'for its own sake' is irrelevant compared to 'what you need to know to stop yourself being fooled and manipulated'. But once their expectations of what can be achieved is expanded, the demand for really useful knowledge increases accordingly.

I no longer accept any viewpoint on any subject without working it out for myself and I have discovered I believe quite different things from the beliefs I've had thrust upon me in the past — mainly by men.

The link between knowledge and change is difficult to measure in a course as young as ours, and of course the experience of Second Chance is only one small thread in an incredibly complex web which is women's consciousness and existence. But whilst a course on medieval history or conversational French or yoga may, for specific reasons and in certain circumstances be highly significant to a particular individual, it is not usual for such classes (or even adult O and A-level courses) to have a general and major impact on virtually all the participants.

At a personal level several women have escaped the independence on anti-depressants and tranquilisers as a way of getting through the week, and some consciously have done away with make-up, long hair and high heels as symbols of the things which men like and which they had previously worn 'to please'. The confidence to be yourself and to dress and look the way you want is perhaps a small step, but a significant one, in the personal politics of women's liberation.

Others have found friendship and support in the group which has gone some way to redressing the isolation from each other that many women are made to accept.

I've gained the friendship and support of some wonderful women and probably learned as much from them as from the course as such — I can't really separate the two!

Apart from the real pleasure of learning and realising I have capabilities, the most enjoyable aspect for me has probably been the closeness and friendship of a group of women.

I now look at women as members of the same sex instead of individual units attached to men and can see with great pleasure the love, support and enormous fun we can get from being together. I really didn't know that this was possible before — not because women weren't capable — but because somehow women are always separated once they're married.

I've changed my attitude to men and women a lot. Now I find it increasingly hard to spend time with men without getting ratty and restive — not because I dislike them particularly but because they seem a waste of space. When I go out with a crowd I monopolise the women — much to their chagrin — if they want to chat up the blokes there's no chance! Also some of the women I've know for years and always dismissed as boring — I now spend more time with them than the men I actually like. Most odd! (I have to tell you that there are a lot of glassy-eyed confused women stumbling around the pubs of Southampton in retreat!) I just increasingly find women more interesting and I really like to spend time with them.

It's a great feeling between the women and just goes to show that women can support each other very effectively despite opinions to the contrary. Personally I'd rather spend time with Second Chance women than with men.

Again it is possible to attach too much significance to the long phone calls, the shared visits, the parties and evenings at the pubs, the exchange of goods and looking after each others children — except to say that we jokingly have come to speak of all these things as indicative of 'sisterhood', and perhaps the term has acquired a new dimension in the process. Certainly, the social nature of the course has become increasingly important as it has developed, and by this I don't mean social/recreational, I mean shared learning and solidarity with others, which is something very different from the individualism encouraged by traditional education. Both Willis[27] and Keddie have argued strongly that the dominant ideology of individualism in education runs contrary to many of the strongest aspects of working-class culture. For Keddie

the issues is not whether individuals have needs or whether they should be met but *how those needs are socially and politically constituted and understood, how they are articulated and whose voice is heard.* Adult education responds to the collective voice of individualism (understood and contexted only with the cultural bias of individual achievement and middle-class life-styles) but has to a large measure failed to identify with the needs of those who reject the premises on which individualism is based.[28] (Keddie's italics)

And of course we should not be surprised that, given the opportunity, women discover that they actually like each other. Friendship between women is not new although the spread of capitalist relations and the intensification of patriarchal attitudes during the last hundred years or so have taken their toll. The ubiquity of family-centred ideology and the compulsory nature of heterosexist coupling has frequently conspired to keep women separate from each other as friends and allies. For some of the male friends and husbands of women on the course the increasing commitment of women to each other has been both curious and threatening. A few women have discovered that they are also capable of loving each other, that their sexuality is their own creation rather than something to be received unquestioningly in response to men, and that 'alternative lifestyles, sex and politics are not merely the concerns of a shifty, threatening minority' — a realisation which has clearly aroused feelings of confusion, anxiety and conflict in the process of becoming accepted and resolved.

Others who would not think in terms of love between women have none the less reviewed the extent to which their future happiness necessarily relies on relationships with men. For many, Second Chance has been accompanied by some degree of stock-taking in terms of personal relationships, especially when family and friends have been less than supportive.

My studying is looked upon as a little hobby; alright as long as it doesn't interfere with wash day and baking day.

I don't always find that family, etc., are really behind me.

My husband was pleased that I was accepted for the Second Chance course, but then I discovered the 'woman's role in society', my attitude changed towards everyday things and his attitude changed towards Second Chance . . . He would usually sulk or be very difficult the evening before I was due to attend.

He pays lip service to it being a good idea, but then complains about the meal, the housework and my 'head in the clouds attitude to life'. He always puts me down, belittling my efforts at writing . . .

I think my parents and parents-in-law quite liked me in the role of 'the little woman' and they are distinctly unhappy about my idea of going to university full time.

Sometimes it's hard to admit you're a feminist when they use 'women's lib' and 'lesbian' like terms of abuse.

My husband — well at first he thought the course was a good idea. I think he thought it would give me something to think about (it certainly did that) and would stop me complaining about my lack of outside interests. About four weeks into the course he changed his mind. The topic we were covering in those first few weeks could have a lot to do with it — women's suffrage. I can smile now at my zealousness. Because of my new 'awareness' I was walking round with an invisible soap box under my arm championing women's rights. Anyone who stood still long enough got their ears bent about the injustices that had been inflicted on women, by men, for centuries, (Oh dear, I'm off again). Anyway this caused a few problems.

Relationships with family and friends have become increasingly difficult — coming home from the course is increasingly difficult — it's almost like schizophrenia. While I'm amongst Second Chance women I feel alive — coming home requires a complete change of personality which is more and more difficult to cope with. As the course takes up more and more time the attitudes and beliefs which come from it are now constantly with me causing constant strain and aggravation in my marriage — probably because I'm always so pre-occupied.

None of my family are interested. Apart from the first few weeks of the course when my Mum asked what I was doing (and it was painfully obvious that she wasn't really interested) none of them want to know, not even my two sisters. I hardly see my Dad, although that wouldn't make much difference anyway. Still, what's new? My husband is 200 per cent against it: the only interest he shows is to start an argument. Half way through the course he seemed to resign himself to the fact that I would go anyway, and even managed to ask a few questions occasionally (nothing more than requiring a 'yes' or 'no' but it was a start). He resents and belittles my learning. If we have a disagreement his stock answer, particularly when proved wrong, is 'And I suppose you learned that at school?' Matters have worsened now that its nearing the end of the course. He feels threatened that I am going to further my education, especially with a career in mind and we have constant arguments about being 'too big for my boots' and about money now that he knows I've applied for the poly. Talk about getting your five eggs in first. He doesn't yet know that I've been accepted (great eh?) and already he's informed me that he won't sign anything, or allow me to show his audited accounts to apply for a grant, nor give me even a penny towards travelling or books. (I'm trying not to worry about this yet, you never know, he might have a brainstorm or something) I have only one friend who shows real interest and encouragement apart from women on the course. In fact she's the only one outside Second Chance who knows that I've been accepted. I'm not saying that other friends are indifferent, it's just that they can't understand. They think I'm mad to want to go back to school. They ask why but I know it's useless to try and explain too deeply because they don't *feel* that way yet.

For students experiencing disharmony and stress in relationships at home the tendency can be to blame the course. The stress may be no greater than that which is experienced by many mature students when they return to study and begin to define themselves differently in relation to their family and friends. Probably it is no greater than the disharmony and stress which characterises countless domestic relationships in which women have not re-examined their lives in feminist terms. But it is often easier to be wise about this after the event. Barbara Hancock comments,

By its very nature the 'oppressive reality' of women is highly personal and hidden. The action of trade unionists against their bosses is far more obvious and public. Action for a woman is far more subtle. Its obvious and extreme point would be where a woman's learning gave her the self-understanding and confidence to leave a husband who was beating her. But for many women the reality is much more subtle. Their problem, their oppressor, is often not a husband who is physically maltreating them. It is an oppressive set of assumptions, which may be shared by any or all of her family, her friends and the society around her. These assumptions define women's lives and futures in a way that denies them their full humanity. They are denied the chance to explore and develop their full potential. These assumptions about women's role are wrapped up in the ordering of power and privilege in society and can be summed up in the phrase 'a woman's place is in the home'. Western capitalist society needs a certain kind of family, with particular roles in those families. In Britain, women's work outside the home is needed at some times (e.g. in war or in the boom in the 60s) but not in other times (e.g. now). Women's work in the home is needed in our economic system so that men may work outside it and so those who are not economically active — children and sometimes the handicapped or the elderly — are cared for. In order to overcome the usual assumptions about her role, a woman has first to establish that she's got a right to a life outside of that focused purely on the needs of other people. A woman may join a mother and toddler club, a slimming club, a macrame class, or a women's circle with visiting speakers who give cookery demonstrations, or even take a part time job to keep the family out of debt. But all of these activities are 'safe' — they make no challenge to her home-focused life, as well, these activities are in any case home focused in one way or other. Joining a political party, or taking a course in maths provide more of a challenge to her assumed role. And Second Chance is even more of a challenge, as it clearly stands for an offer of a new way of life — a life in which the home is not the only focus, and is not the only way in which she can find her identity. Both working-class and middle-class women may have to take a stand to assert their individuality and rights as a person independent from those who depend on them. Working-class women, though, have a double disadvantage. A middle-class woman is more likely to have the resources (through her husband's income or her own earning potential) to find good child care. For her a 'return to work' could well mean return to a satisfying worthwhile job. A working-class woman's job options are much more limited. Paying for child care is a problem, and does working all day on a supermarket check-out expand a woman's individuality and identity? Hence education becomes a crucial element in seeking a new life for working-class women. It expands the possible options and makes it possible to hope not only for a life beyond the home but for a life in which it's possible to contribute in a meaningful way in her own right to society, not merely through what her husband or children may achieve.

The foregoing is not meant to denigrate the home and the undoubted satisfaction and purpose which the raising of children gives many women. The criticism is of the pressures from society which close other options to women, making many experience the home as a trap.[29]

Some begin to resolve these dilemmas by separating from the marriages which seem to symbolise and perpetuate 'the trap'. Others, whose relationships with men are not simply oppressive but based on a good deal of understanding, shared commitment to children and mutual support, seem able to renegotiate the relationships to take account of their changing perceptions of themselves.

This course has made me think and question almost everything, which I think is a very good thing because the ideas and relationships which stand up to the questioning seem now more important to me.

By helping me to see my own life and society in general in a different way, the course has helped me to revalue myself and my relationship with my husband. Before Second Chance I considered myself a failure, not only academically but in personal relationships in life generally. I always thought my inability to be content in the traditional role of wife and mother and my failures in those areas were due to some defect in my character — my personal failure as a woman. I am now more inclined to believe that considering that it is impossible to be the perfect wife and mother I haven't done such a bad job, and that my discontent is not my personal problem but inevitable in a society which robs women of their individuality and pushes them into restricted stereotyped roles.
My relationship with my husband has improved considerably and now I appreciate him and value our marriage more highly than I have for many years. In the past he has always disliked me having any interests or activities which did not include him and expected my whole world to revolve round him as though I were not really a person but some kind of possession. I thought his attitudes selfish and strongly resented his attempts to restrict my independence. Over the last year I have come to see my husband is also a victim of social conditioning and my resentment towards him personally has diminished. Though I don't agree with his

views, I now understand better why he holds them and I have become more tolerant. His attitude to me has also changed, he now seems to accept that I have a right to interests and ambitions of my own and was even supportive during a recent 'confidence crisis' on my part. This change of attitude must have meant a difficult adjustment on his part and I have gained a new respect for him as a person.

Although many women have been able to revalue and reconstruct their relationships at home in a positive way, others have become increasingly aware of the contradictions which made some of these relationships unbearable. To be able to clarify what is wrong, with a view to making changes instead of accepting frustration and guilt as personal failure, also represents a positive development, although when this is experienced in relation to a course like ours there is a danger that we are blamed for the dislocation in personal relationships that can occur. These criticisms have to be anticipated and discussed publicly. More significant would be the failure to support students during their attempts to achieve some kind of personal praxis, so that the usual demarcation between tutor and student and course time and non-course time has effectively to be removed — a difficult principle to argue with those who organise courses according to a strict free-enrolment economy and with implicit notions of hierarchy and detachment. And in this respect the continued involvement of women in the course represents action of a fundamental kind — not in the sense of visible protest so much as in the meaning implied by their involvement. For everyone, to a greater or lesser extent, and in a more-or-less painful way, the action of going through Second Chance means taking a stand about their lives and having the resolve to do things quite contrary to the prevailing assumptions of family, friends and the society around them. And it would be wrong to assume that those who are technically 'tutors' are any more immune to these consequences than others. It would be strange to find a programme of reciprocal learning with this degree of mutual involvement as being one in which some rather than others have all the answers, and who by virtue of being 'teachers' are not equally engaged in the difficult process of reflection, reaction and re-creation.

For some students enthusiasm about the course is considerably less than the picture presented so far might suggest. Their reservations and objections provide important considerations which should not be overlooked, although in the context of the course as a whole, they represent a minority view. One student, who could possibly be described as 'aspiring working class' in the classic sense, and married to a very dominant and conservative husband, made much of the question of bias — by which she meant that the views of the tutors were obviously socialist. Others have considered the course too political, too feminist and in danger of being anti-men. Of course some women do have fairly low opinions of men and do not need the course to incite these feelings. And it would be difficult to examine the historical and pervasive oppression of women within patriarchy without adopting a more critical perspective on the assumptions and behaviour of men than is commonly the case. But some students explain things in socialist terms and take the view that men are also the recipients of class oppression. Others argue a sociological position which depicts men as the victims of social conditioning into certain attitudes and practices. The extent to which women choose to blame or excuse men varies enormously according to the feelings and experiences and perceptions of different women, but probably most of them become convinced that they should collude less, and demand more, in the way of respect and proper recognition.

I seem to have arrived in my mind instead of floundering somewhere. I don't seem to need men's approval so much and can see myself and my desires as being as important as anyone elses, and completely valid.

My advice to anyone contemplating a course like Second Chance is to do it — absorb everything, make up your own mind — but stick with it. It will help you to find yourself, value yourself and give you the confidence to be yourself.

As tutors, our broad commitment to a more egalitarian and just society including the principles of feminism are something none of us would wish to deny, and most students resent the suggestion that they are vulnerable to our indoctrination as a consequence of this. One or two who do not think of themselves as working class may feel some discomfort about the concentration on working-class issues, but then others take delight in the term being used with positive as distinct from pejorative connotations. Fears about indoctrination and encouraging 'over-robust attitudes to securing women's rights' were criticisms taken up in anonymous letters from members of the general public and in enquiries from a local councillor and chairman of the educational advisory panel, the area education officer and the chairman of the local ratepayers' association. The fact that our students are adults and not children seemed to be ignored by these careful watchdogs, and the foolishness which encouraged the local county councillor and chairman of the educational advisory panel to enquire about our 'inciting women to use bad language' seemed to escape none but them.

It is easy to dismiss objections like this, but it is worth remembering that in the battle against marginality, complaints of this nature would not even be investigated normally, nor would allegations of political bias be levelled against any of the countless so-called neutral courses which celebrate the assumptions, achievements and concerns of mainstream culture. Imagine a geography or a literature or an archeology tutor being accused of encouraging 'an over-robust enthusiasm' for the subject!

One or two students each year certainly find the course content threatening — though most of them prefer to make a distinction between challenging and threatening,

> I have found many of the ideas and questions challenging to me personally. They totally contradict many of the beliefs I was brought up with and still live with to a certain extent. I don't know how these contradictions will be resolved but I think that it's a good thing to be forced to face the realities . . . I haven't found any of it threatening.

> Yes a challenge to my deadened mind but threatening, no, why should it be?

> Challenging, yes, threatening, of course not — I have a mind of my own.

> Yes, I have found the issues raised by the course personally challenging and to some extent threatening. Even communicating with others is a personal challenge after 11 years at home!

> Life at home with the housework and the children for company, although busy, can dull the senses and becoming aware and getting involved with the issues affecting women today can be

quite a shock. A lot of values and attitudes are bound to be challenged when you leave the security of home and begin to look outside again.

But for those women married to men who are accustomed to expecting little but domesticity from their wives, and women who have developed an emotional and social dependence on their traditional roles, a critical examination of these can also be threatening. Practical feminism, sisterhood and solidarity with other women has been a central bond which has united most students and tutors but, as you might expect, it has offended others. After all, not all students, for reasons we all know about, define their social and economic condition in quite these terms. As Martin Yarnit comments in relation to working-class students in Liverpool,

[our course] has always had to come to terms with the tension between the interests of the politically committed who form a coherent and vocal minority of the students, and the needs of often minimally class-conscious students. We have recognised the advantages . . . of this mix but we also hold that adult education for the working class has to offer stimulus to both the committed and the uncommitted.[30]

As in Liverpool, most of our students seem to identify to a greater or lesser extent with the aims and purpose of our course, but it is important that they should all feel at ease in discussing them. Inevitably, in a course like Second Chance these issues are controversial, and unlike the 'hidden political curriculum' of most adult education provision, they are more explicit. We have not lost a spattering of students each year by default or because it was raining or because their lift did not arrive or because they had decided to try pottery instead, but because they knew the implications of what they are learning from us and from each other and it proved objectionable to them.

No one engaged in this kind of work must underestimate the significance of this, but should be aware that it is a dilemma which is seldom recognised or faced by those preoccupied with conventional provision.

In the end, as adults, our students will make up their own minds. To assume that they need protection from controversy is patronising, and to avoid a free and open debate about social and political concerns is to deny the central importance of these in the organisation of society. A women from the 1981 course puts it like this,

> I often wonder what I would have been doing now if I hadn't had this Second Chance — and I can tell you in all honesty — the answer I came up with made me feel very uncomfortable.

Hopefully, subsequent groups of students will continue to welcome the same opportunity and continue to thrive upon it.

Inter-agency Co-operation

In addition to Second Chance a further development over the last three years or so has been to increase and expand the women's education programme offered by the University, the WEA and the LEA. Our intention has been to work towards a comprehensive educational provision which combines the resources of separate providers, and in which the demarcation between 'more academic' and 'less academic' provision becomes meaningless. In our experience women who attend our classes are much less interested in who has the responsibility for providing them, than about what they offer and about the context in which useful learning takes place. So far as students are concerned courses we provide about, for example, law, local politics, women's writing, maths, female sexuality, unemployment, motor mechanics, trade union rights, statistics, sexism in education, women's health issues, study skills, women's history, feminist art, radio and video workshops and the like, all originate from the same source and operate in the context of a vision of women's education which is comprehensive, flexible and accessible. It is a vision which takes women's right to education seriously, and which is concerned to validate women as a group with special interests to defend and promote.

The philosophy is less easy to sustain among professionals, however, especially those whose professional rivalry is sustained by careful lines of demarcation between providers. It is a philosophy which I suspect will only work in circumstances in which knowledge is not compartmentalised and organised hierarchically, and in which the concern of providers is determined principally by what makes sense to students rather than what has come to be the declared conventions of institutions. The extent to which we have succeeded in blurring the boundaries between providers and have been able to discount institutional rivalries and competition for students, has been slight. It has enabled us to develop grass-roots co-operation across University/LEA boundaries within the Women's Studies programme, but has been the cause of considerable tension back in our separate institutions (about who pays the tutors, who received the fees, who produces publicity and who answers enquiries from the general public). It has provided no serious models of good practice and inter-agency co-operation which other subject or interest groups within our separate institutions have seen the value of pursuing. The continual frustration of adminstrative rules and institutional constraints which effectively limit, restrict and neutralise attempts to achieve some kind of multi-disiplinary wholeness in the provision of women's education, has encouraged us to move towards increasing our independence from what are essentially the regulations designed to perpetuate patriarchal educational systems. We have done this in Southampton by establishing a Women's Education Centre.

The Women's Educational Centre

The Women's Education Centre was opened in 1981 in a large Victorian classroom used, until the previous summer, as a 'School of Cookery'. The cookers, benches and sinks were removed and the delapidated and dingy mess that remained was plastered and decorated, and cleaned and furnished by women already involved in the women's education programme. The second phase of the centre — a disused three-bedroomed house attached to the newly transformed 'Women's Room' — became the subject of long negotiations with its owners, Hampshire County Council, and a year later it was agreed to open it up, rewire it, and make it structurally safe so that we could furnish and decorate it and add it to the women's room to complete the Women's Education Centre.

The Centre is the first of its kind in the country in that it belongs to a single provider, the LEA, but acts as a focus for a comprehensive programme of women's education sponsored partly by public bodies and partly by independent resources. The Centre is organised by a collective of its members who operate as a voluntary organisation which has raised independent funds, and which is seeking grants from charitable and educational trusts. The Women's Education Centre Collective plans the Centre activities and promotes the courses, workshops, meetings and conferences which members want in co-operation with representatives from the University, the LEA and the WEA. Anyone who attends the Centre can attend general planning meetings, and be as involved as they like in suggesting and participating in activities. Many of the groups meeting in the Centre are self-programming, we have a Centre newsletter which acts as a focus for communication, and as the second phase of the building becomes available we shall be able to expand the facilities and respond to more ideas for appropriate activities and action. The Centre will also provide crèche facilities, a resources library, a herstory archive and as much equipment as we can acquire to become increasingly self-reliant in terms of producing publicity material and printing our own publications.

At any one time women will be able to come to the Centre to take part in courses, get involved in the process of creating and building and developing the Centre as an exciting and expanding adventure, find confirmation and support from other women and share skills and knowledge with others who will join us in the future. We have the opportunity to provide not only a programme of women's education which is a reflection of women's experience and knowledge, culture and political concerns, but also to create a social and emotional environment which can celebrate and confirm collective and feminist principles as a real alternative to hierarchical and patriarchal relationships.

It remains to be seen, however, in the work we still have to do in this direction, whether our autonomy will be respected, and whether our achievements will have any lasting influence on the general provision of adult education for women in the future.

Institutional Reactions

The problem with most post-war liberal adult education which emanates from university extramural departments and local education authorities like ours is that, in general, it has concentrated on intellectual and recreational needs alone, and has consistently failed to relate itself to the social and economic conditions which influence and shape the lives of ordinary people. This is one of the main reasons why it has failed to involve working-class students in any significant numbers. There are other reasons too,[31] but in the end most of them come up against the apparent unwillingness of adult education to look critically at its own practices and to prefer explanations about working-class alienation which concentrate on the limitations of working-class students who do not 'take advantage of what we have to offer'.

According to Keith Jackson, even liberal progressives have failed,

> not because they set themselves a social purpose . . . but because they reduced that purpose to a largely educational affair, thus losing most of its meaning in material terms for ordinary men and women.[32]

For those of us working in the liberal sector or adult education, the urgency is to review continually our educational practice in the light of theory — not a purely educational theory which examines education in isolation from its social context — but a careful examination of the relationship between education and social and political analysis. In this way our practice should be dynamic, continually developed and carefully re-examined.

To attempt this process of praxis and to expand and improve courses like Second Chance and developments like the Women's Education Centre is only part of the matter, however. In the last resort the significance of what we do and its meaning to women — its strengths and weaknesses and struggles — measured only in terms *of itself* assumes that the issues raised can be confined *within* the boundaries of women's studies. The issues raised by work like ours — and I have commented on some of them in this chapter — should be faced just as centrally by education generally. So long as the process of critical re-examination does not penetrate the most prestigious forms of education, we are in danger of assuming that their practices are sacrosanct, and that problems lie only in those areas of provision like ours which operate on the fringes of educational concern.

The usual institutional responses to Second Chance have been to recognise and value those aspects of the course which can most easily and satisfactorily be incorporated into the public ideologies of general provision. The over-subscription of women anxious to do the course each year gets noticed in a world in which numbers count. The extent to which others in different parts of the country, independent funding bodies, conferences, the media and the educational press have shown interest in the course has for all the wrong reasons, reduced our vulnerability to local investigations and criticisms. And, of course, the enthusiasm for learning which is reinforced by the experience of the course, and which encourages several women each year to apply to be full-time students, sets 'the seal of approval' on 'the propriety' of our work. It is interesting that, although Second Chance is not principally concerned to feed higher education institutions with mature students, and although in soliciting student reactions to the course, this is not, as we have seen, the outcome which they particularly stress; so far as the university is concerned, the reservations which colleagues obviously have about the work in general are suspended so long as tangible achievements of this kind can be registered. In this respect we are secure. For as long as a concern about 'continuing education' in other institutions remains strong, the link through us to intelligent, committed, highly motivated and already educationally engaged students is obviously appealing. And many of our students — despite their previous experiences of education — are, not surprisingly to us, quite capable of taking on the kinds of studies which colleges, polytechnics and universities provide. There is no doubt that as long as places are available we shall have a number of women each year choosing to fill them. Women who may have begun the course looking for an O-level, or hoping that an interest outside the home will stop them going scatty, will in the process of discovering their capabilities and reviewing their prospects find that they can be taken seriously as 'proper' full-time students.

But herein lies the dilemma. For women who have no qualifications, no prospects of anything other than low-paid, unskilled and uninteresting jobs, few financial resources, and who frequently live within assumptions that keep them locked into domesticity, the prospects of further or higher education can appear to be a liberating release. To actually be paid more on a grant as a student than you actually earn in a part-time job, or to discover that instead of cleaning the university or child-minding for its students, you can actually study there in your own right, seems as close to some as Utopia. And yet everything I have previously said about patriarchal education still holds true. However enthusiastic about Second Chance students, individuals within the local technical college, colleges of higher education, the polytechnic and the university might be, these institutions remain steeped in patriarchal assumptions about knowledge, about learning and about society in general. Few of them make any allowances for the additional responsibilities which mature students usually have in terms of providing crèche facilities or half-term play schemes for school-age children. Lectures and seminars are arranged to suit the convenience of the timetable and not women with family commitments. For many working-class students an introduction to the cultural elitism or cultural separatism of essentially middle-class establishments can be oppressive. The general assumptions that 'normal students' are eighteen or so can be paternalistic. The concentration on the competitive individualism of assessment, examinations and measurable achievement is totally at odds with the collective and non-competitive atmosphere of Second Chance. It would be comforting to believe that Second Chance, one day a week for three terms, and despite a previous history of educational alienation and the destruction of self-confidence, is long enough and strong enough for women to discover both an enthusiasm for learning and the courage and resolve to later withstand the strictures and values of patriarchal practices in higher education. Maybe as more of our students go together into the same courses and confront the same pressures together, they will be better able to take a stand against them. But for those whose only experience of serious study is within the supportive, feminist and non-competitive context of Second Chance, the shock of discovery that not all education is the same can be overwhelming for individuals facing it alone.

Early signs are that some at least are rising to the battle and challenging the implicit sexism of some of the teaching they are receiving. Others (although unnecessarily overawed a lot of the time) retain a spritely irreverence which hopefully will see them through.

At the tech we learned about Durkheim (a bit like the scarlet pimpernel — always popping up everywhere) and Parsons who thinks we want law and order, and Marx who thinks we all want revolution, and about structuralists, and functionalists, and pluralists and best of all about deviants (although I don't think we were actually supposed to turn out as deviants) and Sylvia who just wants us to write an essay.

In QMD (Quantitative Methods for Dunces or, as it is known in the trade, Quite Mindblowing Drivel) we do survey methodology. The most important method seems to be cluster sampling. We tried it on the grapes in Tesco and got a slap from the manager for our trouble. We did significance levels too, and we know that the significance is significant if its significance signifies a significantly significant significance — the trouble is we ain't got a clue what the significance signifies — and if we did, would we care?

When I started at the poly I did suffer from culture shock and panic attacks at first, not forgetting eyestrain and writer's cramp. 'Rationalism' meant nothing to me and Weber was a neighbour I used to know. The language used by lecturers is still rather strange and a scrambler is a definite advantage, but once you realise that intellectualism is just an excuse for an ego trip you're alright. At present my grant is £2,700 a year plus £370 travelling expenses and is definitely better than work/social security. Now I'm only answerable to myself for what I spend the money on — no social security snoopers, no loss of pay through illness — just extra hard work to catch up from someone else's notes.

In psychology we learned about Skinner — he put pigeons in little boxes and fed them if they pressed the bar. We thought we'd test out his theories by shutting the kids in the shed but we kept forgetting to feed them at the appropriate moment and Mrs. Snodgrass up the road called in the NSPCC. (Some people fail to realise the vital importance of psychological experiments). However, we are beginning to wonder if all the important stuff is done in secret at lunchtime when all the working-class students are up the refectory eating their peas off their knives.[33]

Despite the jokes, it is easy to see how further and higher education returns students to 'the real business' of studying men and how the radical concerns of a course like Second Chance can easily become incorporated by the institutions which control us, because it is easier in the end to comply with, rather than take a stand against, prevailing values. It is even appealing to imagine that we can make the system work for us rather than against us. In the short term, a system working 'for us' rather than 'against us' is arguably preferable to exclusion and oppression, and there are those who would no doubt argue that continual negotiation and confrontation within systems will lead to their modification and change.

In terms of adult education, as in all social institutions which negotiate the struggle between conflicting class and cultural interests, the possibility of change is ever-present. Policies and programmes are not made in heaven: they are made among men; and the evidence that women, conscious of their feminist interests, are now entering this debate is bound to have significant repercussions in terms of the distribution of resources and on the nature of what gets provided. To some extent we have found this to be a part of our experience in Southampton. Each year since 1979 the Women's Studies programme has expanded, and more resources have been committed to it despite the general cuts in spending. By definition, then, we have succeeded in redistributing resources to women's education and working-class students which would previously have been used to promote the traditional programme. There is rather less evidence, though, that the content and continuation of that which remains has learned anything from our experience.

Maralyn Frye, writing about Women's Studies developments inside American colleges and universities, has described the extent to which attempts to reform patriarchal education systems from within are fruitless, and how the freedom to develop the skills and the courage necessary to transform our own sense of ourselves as women, as well as our relationships with men, is only really possible outside of men's institutions.[34] As we have seen, greater access to men's education in educational institutions created and controlled by men, without profound changes in these institutions, will only teach women more about subordination. If women are to anticipate equality in a society in which our inequality is institutionalised both in public bodies and in private relationships which reflect patriarchal attitudes, the need for a separate physical and symbolic space for women, in which we can learn from each other's experience, clarify our needs and our rights, confirm our allegiances and prepare for our possibilities, is of paramount importance.

Whatever strengths we can develop in this way will, for most women, have to be taken back into personal, economic and social relationships with men — and in educational terms, into the very institutions which so conspicuously mistreat us. Since these institutions and relationships must also ultimately be transformed, it is important not to cut our links with them completely. If it is possible for us as women to win space and control over our own education, which can take place as an alternative to, and exist alongside, the education which men have to offer us — but in a way which requires men to take some responsibility for what happens and which requires them to take seriously the political social and cultural arguments about why such separate provision is necessary — then we have the possibility of combining freedom from patriarchal control with the opportunity to develop some alternatives which can provide ammunition for those who also wish to transform conventional provision. If — as we are told — the provision of adult education is generally in the hands of those anxious to respond to the collective voices of women who are clear about our needs and our expectations, there should be no shortage of support for developments which enable us to control our own learning in this way and to accept as valid, a sensible and serious alternative to the education which has hitherto denied us much validity.

Notes

1. See, e.g. Martin Yarnit, 'Second Chance to Learn, Liverpool; Class and Adult Education'; David Evans, 'Writers Workshops and Working Class Culture', and the Forword by Keith Jackson, all in J. L. Thompson (ed.) *Adult Education for a Change*, Hutchinson, 1980.

2. See, e.g. P. Fordham, G. Poulton, L. Randle, *Learning Networks in Adult Education*, RKP, 1979.

3. Peter Clyne, *The Disadvantaged Adult*, Longman, 1972.

4. Coventry CDP Final Report (1975).

5. Fordham *et al., Learning Networks.*

6. Ibid.

7. For example short courses for Asian women bakery workers, women cleaners at Esso Petrol Refinery, and local authority dinner ladies and ancillary workers.

8. Annamarie Wolpe and Annette Kuhn (eds) *Feminism and Materialism*, RKP, 1978.

9. Recruitment procedures for the 1980–1 courses had to be stopped prematurely when the numbers of enquiries had passed 305 and the number of applications had reached 156. We were able to offer places to only 41 students during this academic year.

10. See p. 85.

11. Jane L. Thompson, 'Adult Education and the Disadvantaged', in Thompson (ed.) *Adult Education for a Change.*

12. Nell Keddie, 'Adult Education: An ideology of Individualism', ibid.

13. Sheila Rowbotham, Lynne Segal and Hilary Wainwright, *Beyond the Fragments*, Merlin Press, 1978.

14. Tessa Blackstone, 'The Education of Girls Today', in Juliet Mitchell and Ann Oakley (eds) *The Rights and Wrongs of Women*, Penguin, 1976.

15. Rosemary Deem, *Women and Schooling*, RKP, 1978.

16. Basil Bernstein, 'On the Classification and Framing of Educational Knowledge', in Michael F. D. Young (ed.) *Knowledge and Control*, Collier-Macmillan, 1971.

17. Sue Atkins, 'Law and the Challenge to Patriarchy', in *Women, Class and Adult Education*, University of Southampton, 1981.

18. Jill Mathews, in *Words in Edgeways*, Southampton Women's Education Centre, 1980.

19. Marj Ross, in *On Second Thoughts*, Southampton Women's Education Centre, 1981.

20. Anne Chase, in *Words in Edgeways*.

21. Barbara Hancock, personal evaluation of 1980–1 Second Chance courses.

22. Anne Farwell in *On Second Thoughts*.

23. Julia Kellaway, 'Words in Edgeways', in *Women, Class and Adult Education*.

24. Publications include: *Words in Edgeways, On Second Thoughts, Herstory Retold, Look Who's Holding the Baby* and the monthly magazine/newsletter *Taking Liberties*. Radio tapes include, *Words in Edgeways* (6 half-hour documentaries sponsored by the EOC), *What on Earth* (A four-programme series for children), *Panic Attacks*, and the *Women's Peace Camp*, Greenham Common.

25. K. H. Lawson, 'Community Education; A Critical Assessment', *Adult Education*, vol. 50, no. 1.

26. See page 66.

27. Paul Willis, *Learning to Labour: How Working Class Kids get Working Class Jobs*, Saxon House, 1978.

28. Nell Keddie in Thompson (ed.) *Adult Education for a Change*.

29. Barbara Hancock, personal evaluation of 1980–1 courses.

30. Martin Yarnit, in Thompson (ed.) *Adult Education for a Change*.

31. See Thompson, Keddie and Westwood in ibid.

32. Keith Jackson in his Forword to ibid.

33. *Taking Liberties*, nos. 4 and 5, Southampton Women's Education Centre.

34. See page 125.

11 LIBERATION NOW OR NEVER?

And what of the future? Shall we have liberation for women now — or never? Certainly we have made some important advances in the last decade or so. The idea that women are entitled to equal treatment with men in society is a much less cententious statement today than it was in the early sixties; and a considerable profusion of detailed, systematic, visionary and passionate scholarship has gone into the recovery of our cultural past from the oblivion of masculine history. New theories and fresh interpretations of the social world which take proper account of the experiences of women have emerged; and we begin to understand the pervasive and oppressive implications of sexual power relationships which have made the naming of patriarchy so important in our struggle for radical social change. Governments have been forced to concede legislative reforms, and there has been a general shift in public consciousness about women's rights which did not exist fifteen years ago.

But there is little room for complacency. We have seen how women's energy and bravery and deep conviction about injustices have been denied and neglected as a force in history, leaving each new generation of feminists the task of rediscovery and re-creation. We have seen women punished, slandered and ridiculed for loving women. We have seen anger dismissed as neurosis, and the demand for authentic political integrity described as irrelevant and divisive. In these circumstances we should not expect any favours from powerful men, but recognise the challenge which allegiance and community between women presents to those who have grown accustomed to controlling us. We need now to safeguard our advances, to defend our achievements and to secure our future against the ubiquitous and inevitable reaction of those concerned to insist that 'we protest too much', that 'all is well' and that '*real* women are happy to stay home with their children'.

Neither should we underestimate the power of the fathers — of male lovers, employers, politicians, teachers, scientists, lawyers, priests, journalists, advertisers and the like — determined to divide us against each other. By promoting male values and in defending male interests they continually eclipse our realities and our concerns in ways designed to keep us in the place they have reserved for us. Their strategies — coercive, academic, legalistic and moralistic — take many forms, but their purpose is invariably the same: to prevent us from strengthening our commitment to each other and from claiming our right to love and work together. Divisiveness is a strategy traditionally encouraged by patriarchy which has always split and separated women as virgins or vamps, madonnas or medusas, dutiful daughters or dykes. And in this tradition the contemporary male Left and the purveyors of sexual liberation are scarcely more enlightened than those who have gone before,

> The present-day Left has steadily refused to work on women's issues, to deal with sexual oppression in any but the most shallow, hypocritical terms, to confront its own fear and hatred of women. Instead it continues to attempt to divide lesbians and 'straight' identified women, black and white women, to represent lesbianism as bourgeois decadence and feminism as counter-revolutionary, middle-class trivia; just as men in the black movement have tried to define lesbianism as a 'white woman's problem'. (In this connection I love to think of the independent women silk-workers of China, whom Agnes Smedley described in the 1930s, who refused to marry, lived in female communities, celebrated the birth of daughters with joy, formed secret women's unions in the factories, and were openly attacked as lesbians.)[1] The male-defined 'sexual revolution' of pornography, a multi-billion dollar industry which asserts rape as pleasurable, humiliation as erotic, is also a message to women who relate sexually to men, that they can still be 'normal' whatever degradations they may undergo in the name of heterosexuality. Better to collaborate in male fantasies of sexual violence than to be a lesbian: better to be battered than queer.[2]

In America the challenge to patriarchal authority is being currently defended by the activities of the Moral Majority.

The Moral Majority is a rapidly growing quasi-religious and fundamentalist organisation, presided over by Jerry Falwell, and intended to counter political liberalism. It was part of the conservative force which swept Reagan into power, and has concentrated its particular reactionary political and media evangelism on attacking all those engaged in 'un-American' activities. In this kind of climate the advances won by feminism in the 1970s are clearly under attack. In his best-selling book *Listen America*, published in 1980, Falwell has this to say about family life:

> There are only three institutions God ordained in the Bible: government, the church and the family. The family is the God-ordained institution of the marriage of one man and one woman together for a lifetime with their biological or adopted children. The family is the fundamental building block and the basic unit of our society, and its continued health is a prerequisite for a healthy and prosperous nation. No nation has ever been stronger than the families within her. America's families are her strength and they symbolise the miracle of America . . . But in the past twenty years a tremendous change has taken place. There is a vicious assault upon the American family.[3]

Of course the major assailant, according to Falwell, is the women's movement. This is what he says,

> I believe that at the foundation of the women's liberation movement, there is a minority core of women who were once bored with life, whose real problems are spiritual problems. Many women have never accepted their God-given roles. They live in disobedience to God's laws and have promoted their Godless philosophy throughout our society . . . The feminist movement is unisexual. Feminists desire to eliminate God-given differences that exist between the sexes; that is why they are pro-homosexual and lesbian. In fact it is shocking how many feminists are lesbians. . .
>
> In a drastic departure from the home, more than half of the women in our country are currently employed. Our nation is in serious danger when motherhood is considered a task that is 'unrewarding, unfulfilling and boring'. I believe that a woman's calling to be a wife and mother is the highest calling in the world. My wife is proud to be called a housewife. She is dedicated to making a happy and rich life for us and our three children. She does not consider her life-work of making my life happy and that of loving and shaping the lives of our precious children inconsequential or demeaning. Women who choose to remain in the home should never feel inferior to those working outside, but should know that they are fulfilling God's command.[4]

And in case anyone is in any doubt about the power of arguments like these to transform public fear and anguish about the sort of society America is turning out to be into a series of simplistic, scape-goating explanations about moral decline and the 'infiltration of perverts', then the progress through Congress of the Family Protection Act is worth monitoring. Its intention is to:

Prohibit legal-services money from being used for desegregation litigation, gay-rights litigation, divorce litigation or abortion-funding litigation.

Deny federal aid to schools where teachers are unionized in closed shops or where prayer is prohibited.

Deny federal money to groups presenting homosexuality as an acceptable lifestyle.

Exclude lesbians and gays from The Civil Rights Act of 1964.

Prohibit federal independent action on child abuse, spouse abuse and juvenile delinquency.

Remove schools from jurisdiction of the National Labor Relations Act.

Deny federal money for curriculum on non-traditional sex-roles.

Disqualify the Supreme Court from ruling on cases involving prayer in schools and public buildings and from ruling on restrictions states may set on teachers' qualifications.

Deny food stamps to full-time college students.

Given this kind of backdrop, progress within the white male academy is also fraught with problems.

As we have seen, the years between 1970 and 1980 were years of significant growth in Women's Studies teaching in the United States. In 1975 Florence Howe, a professor at the College of Old Westbury in New York and a tireless campaigner for women's rights during this period, said,

If by 1980 the number of courses and programmes has doubled or trebled, and if in freshman English the students are still reading male writers, and in United States history the students are still studying male culture heroes, wars and male political documents, then we shall have failed in our mission.[5]

Peggy McIntosh of the Wellesley College Centre for Research on Women was insistent that,

The traditional curriculum was designed for the education of white male western leaders in a time of western dominance and economic expansion. A revised curriculum would give both our male students (now a minority) and our women a better preparation for the world in which non-western women of colour are the world's majority, the life of western dominance and expansion is no longer taken for granted, and caretaking roles assigned previously to women and other lower-caste people will be needed on a global scale for human survival.[6]

Early developments also reflected the universities' concern to attract older students into continuing education programmes — many of them women — who would be less likely than eighteen-year-olds to tolerate a curriculum which implied that women did not exist. For many, Women's Studies provided not only information that was identity-confirming, but the support and encouragement needed to sustain the feeling that women had a future worth anticipating.

But despite the high expectations and early enthusiasm, the prospects in the 1980s, in the context of a Reagan administration, falling rolls and financial crisis, mean a continuing fight for survival, rather than further progress towards the decolonisation of male scholarship and educational control. A close look at resources reveals that Women's Studies options are in fact costing the universities very little — approximately $50,000 a year in 1981 as against $500,000 for a traditional department teaching the same number of students. Most of the teachers are women, often part time and frequently without tenure. Their enthusiasm and commitment 'to the cause' has probably more to do with what keeps the courses going than official recognition and sponsorship within the university.

Independent funding from big charitable organisations like Ford, Carnegie and Mellon, which were persuaded in the 1970s in a climate of affirmative action and the government's Education Equity Act to provide a good deal of financial support for Women's Studies — $7.5 million in eight years from the Ford Foundation alone — is now much harder to come by. The Ford Foundation's policy document for the 1980s makes no mention of women in higher education. The backlash policies of the New Right, 'Reaganomics' and financial crisis have all encouraged retreat from the liberal reforms and concessions of the 1970s.

Women are being accused of taking men's jobs and undermining family life by their insistence on working. Because only 17 per cent of American households conform to the nuclear family ideal, women are increasingly being told to stay home where they belong. In these circumstances Women's Studies courses have difficulty gaining ground. Florence Howe, at least, has revised her time-scale until the end of the century to take stock of whether 'the mission' has been accomplished.

In Britain the premiership of Margaret Thatcher has done very little to advance the claims of women either, and whilst the utterings of the conservative government are perhaps not quite so hysterical as those of the Moral Majority, the same sense of family supremacy and female dependency are characteristic of its pronouncements. In 1977 Patrick Jenkin reminded the annual conference of the Conservative Party that the family,

> had been the foundation for virtually every free society known to history. It possesses strength and resilience, not least in adversity. Loyalty to the family ranks highest of all, higher even than loyalty to the state . . . I am told there is now a word for 'latchkey children' in every European language . . . in more and more families mothers are combining earning with homemaking. . . . There is now an elaborate machinery to ensure her equal opportunity, equal pay and equal rights; but I think we ought to stop and ask: where does this leave the family?

Well, in 1979 it meant that only 5 per cent of British households actually conformed to the 'ideal' of working husband, dependent wife and two children widely portrayed as the norm,[7] although the pressure to comply with this myth lives on. As Minister for Social Services in the new Conservative government Jenkin went on to proclaim, 'If the good Lord had intended us all having equal rights to go out to work and to behave equally, you know he really wouldn't have created men and women.'

The consequence for many women presented with feminism as an alternative is to acknowledge its aspirations with both anticipation and anxiety. It is difficult to admit the extent to which one's identity has been manufactured within a concept of male ownership and property, and one's possibilities diminished by the spiritual and social coercion of others. So much so that the notion of oppressive power in male–female relationships which is still one which is resisted by those fearful of its implications and those threatened by its exposure.

But feminist analysis also provides hope, and a vision in which the goal is not merely equality, or civil rights, or tokenism in high places, but the profound transformation of society and of human relationships in which each woman can define her own identity in relation to her own needs, and can claim the right to decide how and when and with whom she expresses her sexuality and chooses to utilise her reproductive powers. And education has an important part to play in this.

Coote and Campbell[8] describe women's liberation as one of the most important political developments of this century, unique in its capacity to both create and be created by change. The commitment of the Women's movement to both personal growth and social transformation implies a dynamic and complex appreciation of social organisation which encompasses an ethical vision of a non-oppressive society with egalitarian practice and public action in both private and social relations.

It is in the nature of feminist politics that it is conducted on many different levels at once. We are struggling to change ourselves, to change society and to change our relation to society. We are struggling within the family, with parents, children, siblings, husbands — to change oppressive relationships, to change patterns of behaviour, and to redistribute labour and wealth. We are fighting against cherished traditions and powerful taboos. We are struggling to assert the value of the roles we already perform, to create new ones for ourselves, and to break into those traditionally reserved for men. We are fighting to improve the material conditions of our lives, and to that end we are fighting for power within trade unions and political organisations, as well as against the vested interests of employers and international capital. As we enter into spheres of activity which are dominated by men, we need to transform these too, if we are to survive without becoming surrogate men. We are struggling to change the values and priorities of men alongside us, as well as the way they conduct themselves — in short, to change the world. All the while, we are fighting to assert our own interpretations of what we are doing and our own definitions of what we are, against the man-made versions, which tend to ridicule, belittle or ignore our efforts and achievements.[9]

So far as education is concerned, the choice in the end is between the same strategic possibilities as those discussed within the women's movement. For those who are separatists the solution is simple, politically important and possibly satisfying in a personal sense. But the solution of separatism both from men in general and from their educational system in particular will only ever be acceptable to a minority of women. As an option it should not be discounted, but in the end most of us will need to confront patriarchal relationships with a view to altering them and liberating both women and men from their restrictions. We women must not lose sight of the fact that we have an equal right to inherit an equal world which takes our concerns equally seriously, but this will be achieved only by a concerted attack upon class domination, patriarchal relations and racism — an attack which will also require the assistance of men.

This is not to underestimate the importance of autonomous action, however. The suggestion that men will readily give priority to securing women's rights, whatever else is on their agenda, has never happened in the past and is unlikely to happen in the future without substantial pressure from women. The frequently held assertion that 'we must educate men', or the naïve assumption that 'if we can only find the right arguments men will come to see the justice of our case and be persuaded' are both views which are notoriously lacking in historical precedent. Debates of these kinds in which men hold power, dominate discussion and operate according to their own values and perceptions and experience, in which only a few are even *trying* to understand, and even fewer prepared to accept the personal consequences that such changes will bring about, are not the forums in which it is easy to advance the kinds of issues elaborated at length in this book. Most men have no intention of changing the ordering of relationships or the institutional practices which have served them well for years unless they have to; and so long as their interests are being well satisfied, they have no reason to voluntarily relinquish power and control. In the education world, men's assumptions, their language, their committees, their policy-making bodies, their academic traditions, their discourses, their definitions of reputable scholarship — all insist that any debate about women be conducted in similar terms: in precisely the terms which feminists now wish to reject. Until we women can reconstitute this tradition and enjoy equal respect within it, simply increasing our accessibility to what it has to offer is largely irrelevant. The only real opportunity of equality for us is to develop our own education tradition alongside men's education, to create the conditions in which as women we can make our own knowledge, become our own teachers and be in control of our own resources. To reverse, in fact, the popular trend towards co-education. From such a basis of strength, development, support and autonomy, it will be more possible to re-negotiate relationships with men in our personal lives and in society generally; to make strategic allegiances where appropriate with those groups, including men, who are concerned to challenge prevailing oppression; and to include men in our activities only when they come to learn, or to offer support, rather than to interfere and control. The strength and confirmation which we women can achieve by taking part in activities in our own right, and building our independence as a valid and viable alternative to subordination and dependence on men, is the most effective preparation I can think of for liberation.

But with all this work to do we are still in the infancy of our revolution. The learning of liberation begins with questions, with the discovery of new identity, with the clarification of anger translated into action, with decisions made to shift a life, go back to paid employment, re-enter education, or leave a marriage, and with the individual courage necessary to make such decisions and to see them through. But it does not end here. In Adrienne Rich's words, feminism

> means resisting the forces in society which say that women should be nice, play safe, have low expectations, drown in love and forget about work, live through others and stay in the places assigned to use.[10]

It means renouncing our submission to the fathers, and recognising that the world they have created for us does not do sufficient justice to our visions. For those of us engaged in learning it means being strong, taking control of our own education and our lives and being determined to do things that others have determined should not be done. It means becoming stronger together and using our energies to give each other courage. It means the refusal to sell our talents and our aspirations short simply to avoid conflict and confrontation, to practise disobedience to the rules and regulations devised by men which define our subordination, and to begin thinking, speaking and acting for ourselves as women accountable to women, and sustained by the responsibility we have to each other to keep on fighting for as long as any of us remains unfree.

Notes

1. Agnes Smedley, *Portraits of Chinese Women in Revolution*, Feminist Press, 1976.

2. Adrienne Rich, 'The Meaning of Our Love for Women is What We Have Constantly to Expand', in *On Lies, Secrets and Silence*, Virago, 1980.

3. Jerry Falwell, *Listen America*, Doubleday/Galilee, 1980.

4. Ibid.

5. Lorna Sage, quoted in 'Women on Course', *The Sunday Times*, August 1981.

6. Ibid.

7. EOC Statistics, *The Facts About Women*.

8. Anna Coote and Beatrix Campbell, *Sweet Freedom*, Picador, 1982.

9. Ibid.

10. Adrienne Rich, 'Claiming an Education', in *On Lies, Secrets and Silence*.

INDEX

Made in the USA
Columbia, SC
26 July 2021